net.savvy

CORWIN
PRESS

The Corwin Press logo—a raven striding across an open book—represents the happy union of courage and learning. We are a professional-level publisher of books and journals for K-12 educators, and we are committed to creating and providing resources that embody these qualities. Corwin's motto is "Success for All Learners."

net.savvy

Building Information Literacy in the Classroom

2nd Edition

Ian Jukes
Anita Dosaj
Bruce Macdonald

CORWIN PRESS, INC.
A Sage Publications Company
Thousand Oaks, California

For information:

CORWIN
PRESS

Corwin Press, Inc.
A Sage Publications Company
2455 Teller Road
Thousand Oaks, California 91320
E-mail: order@corwinpress.com

Sage Publications Ltd.
6 Bonhill Street
London EC2A 4PU
United Kingdom

Sage Publications India Pvt. Ltd.
M-32 Market
Greater Kailash I
New Delhi 110 048 India

Library of Congress Cataloging-in-Publication Data

Jukes, Ian.
    NetSavvy: Building information literacy in the classroom / by Ian
Jukes, Anita Dosaj, and Bruce Macdonald.— 2nd ed.
        p.   cm.
Includes bibliographical references.
ISBN 0-7619-7564-0 (cloth: alk. paper)
ISBN 0-7619-7565-9 (pbk.: alk. paper)
1. Internet (Computer network) in education. 2. Education—Computer
network resources. I. Dosaj, Anita. II. Macdonald, Bruce, 1948– III.
Title.
    LB1044.87 .J84 2000

                                                99-050501

This book is printed on acid-free paper.

        04 05 06 10 9 8 7 6 5 4 3

Production Editor: Denise Santoyo
Editorial Assistant: Kylee Liegl
Typesetter: Technical Typesetting Inc.
Cover Designer: Michelle Lee

Contents

This book is dedicated to all of our parents, both here and departed.

About This Book

This is a book about a better way of learning to use the Internet. The authors propose that teaching, learning, practicing, and mastering information management skills are the essential skills needed to be successful in the Communication Age, an era of high-tech, high-speed, digital fingertip data. This book is for anybody and everybody who has a vested interest in learning.

How the Chapters In This Book Are Organized

This book focuses on a five-stage process for becoming comfortable with accessing, analyzing, and applying information obtained through Internet sites, newsgroups, chat rooms, e-mail, and other Internet resources and becoming Info-Savvy and NetSavvy. It consists of three parts and and three Appendixes.

Part I consists of three chapters: Chapter 1 considers the emergence of the Internet and its impact on society and education. Chapter 2 discusses information overload and its subsequent dysfunctions and proposes a solution. In Chapter 3, the 5As of information literacy are presented, and InfoSavvy and NetSavvy are defined.

Part II is made up of six chapters (Chapters 4 through 9) that present tools for teachers and students designed for and aligned to work with an organized list of information-processing skills for the Internet—the NetSavvy Skills Framework. Chapter 4 introduces the Ten-Minute Lesson Planner, which offers a quick and efficient way of creating NetSavvy lesson plans using the 5As approach to help integrate information literacy skills into any content area of the curriculum. Chapters 5 through 9 present lesson planners for each stage of the 5As NetSavvy process, which include Asking, Accessing, Analyzing, Applying, and Assessing, and student tools that articulate with each of the 5 lesson planners.

Part III is the complete NetSavvy Skills Framework.

Part IV consists of five chapters. Chapters 10 through 14 present five commonly held assumptions about education that constitute major obstacles to implementing NetSavvy and InfoSavvy learning environments. Each chapter deals with one major obstacle and suggests methods for overcoming it.

Finally, three Appendixes are provided. Appendix A supplies blank versions of all the NetSavvy teacher tools, and Appendix B consists of blank versions of all student tools. These may be photocopied and used by teachers to create their own lesson plans or to help design their own tools for implementing NetSavvy lessons. Also included is a reading list in Appendix C.

Acknowledgments

We would like to say thanks to all those who gave us the benefit of their wisdom, experience, and time. Many people have influenced and shaped the beliefs and ideas that are presented in this book. To our partners and children, who supported us as we obsessed with "getting it done," without your understanding, patience, and acceptance, this book would not have been possible. To Ted McCain, whose insights originally sparked the idea. To Kate Matheson, Sara Armstrong, Lisa and Steve Holmes, and Bruce and Wendy McKay, thanks for helping to ignite the fire during the creation of "*NetSavvy* I." To all our friends and colleagues who inspired us with their many perspectives on the future of education your insight was invaluable in helping us to clarify and expand many of the concepts outlined in this book. Our deepest gratitude to all of you for believing in our cause and above all, believing in us. And to Gail McDermott, our eternal gratitude and grumbling for her meticulous and relentless proofreading.

The NetSavvy Skills Framework, Teacher Tools, and Student Tools have been reproduced with permission from the InfoSavvy Group © Copyright, InfoSavvy Group, 2000.

Ian Jukes
Anita Dosaj
Bruce Macdonald

About the Authors

Ian Jukes has been a teacher, school administrator, writer, consultant, university instructor, and keynote speaker. As Associate Director of both Educational Technology Planners and the Thornburg Center for Professional Development, he has worked extensively with school districts, as well as businesses, community organizations and other institutions throughout the world. Ian is also the creator and codeveloper of TechWorks, the nationally acclaimed K-8 technology resource; the coauthor of several books, including his latest, *Windows on the Future*; and a contributing editor for the *Audio Education Journal* and *Technology and Learning*. E-mail address: *ijukes@edtechplanners.com*

Anita Dosaj is a teacher, writer, presenter, workshop facilitator, and keynote speaker whose practical and humorous presentations focus on the everyday issues that elementary and secondary teachers everywhere encounter in an environment of unrelenting change. As Associate Director of Educational Technology Planners, she speaks and consults throughout North America, working with districts and schools to address the many critical issues related to coming to terms with information overload and informational dysfunctions among students and educators. She has written a lengthy series of resource materials related to effective strategies for teaching writing as a process and the integration of writing across the curriculum. She is currently completing her doctorate in educational leadership at Pepperdine University in Los Angeles. E-mail address: *adosaj@edtechplanners.com*

Bruce Macdonald is an award-winning author and historian, who also works as a school teacher, public speaker, community activist, cartographer, graphical designer, and researcher. His commitment to improving the education system for teachers and students has led to his involvement in a number of curriculum reform projects aimed at adults in pre-employment programs. His work in graphical design and cartography reflects his continued interest in processing large amounts of information into a clearly expressed and easily accessible form. E-mail address: *bmacdonald@edtechplanners.com*

For more information, contact us at our Web site: *www.edtechplanners.com*

The world we have created is a product of our thinking. It cannot be changed without changing our thinking.

—Albert Einstein

Part I

The Internet, InfoWhelm, and InfoSavvy

Chapter 1

The Internet in Your Face!

Zero to Sixty in the Blink of an Eye

Just what's going on here? Where did this Internet revolution come from? It seems to have crept up and smacked us right between the eyes. When did all this Internet stuff really begin? How long has it been since those gee-whiz articles about the Internet started popping up everywhere in magazines, in newspapers, and on TV? When did surfing go beyond something that was done outdoors in a bathing suit?

Fast forward to today. The Internet is now the central tool of the Information Age. Every company and every industry in the marketplace understand the critical importance of establishing an on-line presence. Today, business completed over the Internet has become far more lucrative than the combined value of traditional transactions for the oil and steel industries. Internet commerce is growing so quickly that it's plainly only a matter of time before it becomes one of the world's largest economic sectors. The Internet as a full-blown commercial medium has already arrived and will undoubtedly be the driving force for many aspects of our lives in the 21st century.

When Did All of This Start?

It's simple. Although personal computers and telecommunications ceased to be a novelty in the late 1980s, it was only with the introduction of the first Web browser to the Internet in 1995 that things really began to take off. This new software greatly facilitated access by the average person to the huge volume of available information and services on the World Wide Web. At the same time, advances in hardware were facilitating the marriage of computers, communications systems, and multimedia. Bingo!—Overnight everyone had the capacity to be digitally wired together through combined audio, graphics, and video communications services and to have access to e-mail and information networks.

On the human landscape, the arrival of the Information Age is best represented by the emergence of Bill Gates as the most successful businessperson in the history of the world. Only an Information Age could transform a 19-year-old university dropout obsessed with computer software into a middle-aged adult worth more than 100 billion dollars in less than 25 years.

Our Changing World

In our old paper-based world, there were approximately 500,000 words in the English language—roughly the number of words that appeared in the largest dictionary. But in the electronic-based world, we have a truer measure of the number of actual words used by people today—about 10 billion words according to author Paul Gilster! Search engines such as AltaVista use information robots to scan Web sites to compile a single index of all the words accessible in electronic form on the Internet. AltaVista's list comprises about 10 billion different keywords. Incredibly, all of the references to any one of these words is available on the Internet almost instantaneously and at virtually no cost. The search for any single word may yield a list of sources in the form of a dozen, a million, or even 10 million Internet sites, in just a few seconds! Being connected globally, you now have complete access to enormous indexes at warp speed without ever having to be on the deck of the starship *Enterprise*.

Not long ago, if you drove to a major library that contained a few million volumes, you might have time to scan through the indexes of a dozen or so books. And although each book may have contained 200,000 or 300,000 words, each index would list only a few hundred. You might turn up a few dozen hits in a few hours of research. The same search on the Internet could dredge up literally millions of references in a matter of seconds.

As a result, the Information Age brings with it a whole new set of challenges, not the least of which is an overwhelming amount of information—what we like to call InfoWhelm. Futurist Richard Saul Wurman estimates that because of information systems, more than 1.3 trillion new documents are produced each year in the United States alone. The ever-decreasing costs of producing new documents has created a raging torrent of information. Add to this equation that every day, it's estimated that more than 8 billion e-mail messages are sent in the United States alone. As a direct result of the emergence of information systems, the Internet, and other advances in electronic communications, there has been more new information produced in the last 10 years than in the previous 10,000.

Education Is Playing Catch-Up

While the Internet has energized business, education is still struggling to find effective ways to integrate on-line access into curricula. Although there are many exciting examples of the educational uses of Internet resources, the general effect to date has been minimal for most American students.

Much of the problem lies in the fact that the fundamental structure of the Internet clashes with traditional classroom practices. For example, the emergence of an ever-changing, almost organic, information source makes most textbooks obsolete before they are printed. In fact, the Internet and its World Wide Web have fundamentally redefined the manner in which information is presented.

Overnight, we have gone from the linear, logical, text-based presentation of information to interactive documents that contain various combinations of text, graphics, sound, and motion video that can be accessed in a nonlinear manner. Instead of changing traditional educational practices to find new ways to work with and take advantage of this new medium, many educators have simply tried to accommodate the emergence of the Internet without changing their traditional instructional practices. Such an approach greatly underestimates the impact that the Information Age will inevitably have on education.

The Amazing Power of the Internet

For most of recorded history, information could only be conveyed over a distance by a messenger physically traveling that distance. As a result, interactivity between the information sender and the end user was often slow and difficult or even impossible. In the past century many advances have been made in our communications infrastructures. Despite significant advances in research (reading, data collection), in communications (telephone, radio, TV), and in publishing (books, magazines, newspapers), each of these has remained a very separate aspect of information processing and delivery. Until recently, each of these media used different technologies to communicate with their audiences. All this has changed. For the first time in history, the Internet has brought the convergence of powerful research, communication, and publishing tools right into businesses, schools, and even the homes of ordinary people.

Overcoming the Obstacles to Using the Internet

However, there is a problem. The capabilities of the Internet are so new and unique that it's difficult to understand, let alone use, the full potential of this powerful new three-in-one medium. As educators, we face two major challenges:

1. Developing mastery of basic information literacy skills so that users are fluent in the new online medium
2. Creating a viable educational context for integrating online resources and activities into effective instructional practices

Mastery of Basic Information Literacy Skills

New information technologies demand a fundamentally different approach to teaching, learning, and the delivery of curriculum. As an example, suppose a student is asked to write a 500-word essay. If the student has no access to information technologies, writing this essay might involve reading and blending information from two or three sources. New technologies such as the Internet give students access to literally millions of documents. Working through this much material and reducing the information to a 500-word essay requires a different set of thinking skills. The essence of information literacy encompasses processes such as clarifying the task, locating appropriate materials, making decisions related to their authenticity, organizing the ideas, using the information to address real life issues, and then evaluating what has been produced.

Creating an Educational Context

A well-developed understanding of how to effectively use Internet resources within an educational context has not yet emerged. This is hardly surprising given the speed at which information technologies are evolving. It's time for educators to come together to carefully consider how, where, and when the use of this powerful tool can be systematically taught and effectively used to enhance the teaching and learning process. There are on-line resources for virtually every curriculum area. These can provide students with the opportunity to thoughtfully examine a wide range of information and then apply what has been learned to real-time projects, products, and experiences. Infusing Internet access and use into educational practice provides a powerful means for augmenting student learning experiences.

The "Net" Effect on Education

Given the range of resources and the possibilities available, it's easy to understand why many educators believe that access to the Internet can have a profound and positive impact upon education. In reality, however, despite sincere efforts to introduce and integrate computer-based technology and Internet access into classroom practices, several recent surveys indicate that the Net has had surprisingly little effect upon student learning.

As the Information Age penetrates deeper into our lives, affecting each of us in a variety of tangible and intangible ways, many old questions about education and literacy need to be revisited. Whereas we used to talk about what it meant to be literate or illiterate, we now need to ask also, "What does it mean to be informationally literate in the Information Age? What are the skills that a person needs to process the huge amount of available data? What are the skills and competencies that more and more employers are looking for in new employees today?"

If our schools are still at least partly geared to the Industrial Age, how deep does their irrelevancy reach? What aspects of schools and learning need to be changed so that 5 or 10 years from now all of our students are informationally literate and possess skills relevant to the ever-changing marketplace? This book will address these questions, and the answers will define what it means to be InfoSavvy and NetSavvy.

Chapter 2

Understanding InfoWhelm

Information Overload

Have you ever had someone ask you if you had read a new book, and you felt embarrassed because you had not heard of the book, let alone the author? Richard Saul Wurman tells us that there are more than 1,000 books published around the world every day, that a weekday edition of *New York Times* contains more information than someone in the 17th century was likely to come across in a lifetime, and that in 1 year, an average person will read or complete 3,000 notices and forms, read 100 newspapers and 36 magazines, watch 2,463 hours of TV, listen to 730 hours of radio, talk on the telephone for 61 hours, and read 3 books, as well as spend increasing amounts of time surfing the World Wide Web and responding to e-mail.

How has all of this affected you? How many of you feel overwhelmed by the amount of information coming your way? Let's take a short test to see how you have been affected. How many of the following apply to you?

- Do you experience major feelings of guilt over your inability to "keep up" with all of the information flowing into your life?

- Do you ever suffer from a sense that there is "so much to do and so little time to do it in?"

- Do you ever experience a feeling of helplessness in the light of relentless media bombardment?

- Do you encounter increasing information overwhelm and exhaustion from the endless flow of information emanating from newspapers, magazines, TV, radio, e-mail, and the Web?

- Do you have sedimentary piles of information on your desk, by your bedside, or in a drawer that you never seem to be able to get to?

- Do you ever become frustrated with your inability to find exactly the information that's needed?

- Do you frequently end up lurching from one task to the next, suffering from a chronic case of the tyranny of the urgent, the immediate, or the unnecessary?

- Has all of this reduced you to often making things up as you go?

The Diagnosis

If some or all of these symptoms apply to you, then you may be suffering from **information dysfunction disorder** (IDD). If so, welcome to the club! IDD is quickly becoming the unofficial brain syndrome of the Information Age, leading to high levels of stress and feelings of being overwhelmed and overloaded. And if it's like this for us, what's it like for our children?

There are at least three types of information dysfunction disorder: informational oblivion, informational paralysis, and informational dyslexia.

The **informationally oblivious** are unconsciously unaware of their condition. They have been bludgeoned, brainwashed, and anesthetized by information overload into benign acceptance of what they are presented with and view most sources and forms of information equally. As a result, they have a passive, accepting mentality that takes as gospel truth almost anything that comes out of a TV, radio, magazine, or computer. How many of you have been deceived by an urban legend received in an e-mail? Have you ever heard someone say, "It's true, it's true, I saw it on Jerry Springer" (or read it on the Web)?

Many others are consumed by scattered bits of minutiae, passively absorbing unrelated, trivial bits of information about everything they have heard, read, or seen. Information, disinformation, and misinformation blend together into a seamless stream. As a result, people often know more about the latest celebrity scandal than they do about the Constitution or our legal system. Even those things they do know about are often understood only at a superficial level. Is it ignorance or is it apathy? They don't know, and they don't really care.

The **informationally paralyzed** are consciously unaware of personal information deficiencies. They know that they don't know and understand that there is a need for them to be better informed, but they are overcome by the sheer amount of information or are frozen by fear of new technologies. As a result, they don't have the skills, can't use the needed tools, can't find the needed information, are unable to interpret the information that is available, or don't understand new ways of presenting the information.

The **informationally dyslexic** are consciously aware of their information problems. They know what they know and what they don't know. They have some information-searching skills, but these are haphazardly applied because the skills have not been sufficiently refined or properly understood. Thus, they are often not able to repeat successful searches for necessary information because the skills are applied inconsistently. Even when they can find the raw data, they become bogged down because they are often confused as to how to view, process, analyze, authenticate, or apply them or technodrool and technolust sidetrack them. The informationally dyslexic suffer from the illusion that being able to use a Web browser to surf the World Wide Web is the same thing as using the information obtained to achieve a useful purpose. As a result, they often find themselves spinning their tires, unable to go anywhere because the ability to access information does not bring with it an ability to evaluate and apply that information.

What's Going On Here?

The traditional ways of processing data just don't work as well today. This is happening primarily because information systems are generating data at such stupendous rates that we can no longer just memorize and recall everything on demand.

In schools, even just a few years ago, academic success was based primarily on the ability to memorize. The traditional instructional model was teach, test, and turf. Teach the content, test the student's ability to recall the information, and then turf it out to get ready for the next unit of study. In such a situation, is it any wonder that you could take a test on one day and do well, but be tested on the same information a few weeks later and have absolutely no memory of the details?

In the past few years there has been a necessary shift away from equating success primarily with rote learning because of the sheer volume of information that is being generated. As a result of the shift, there has been a rapid depreciation in the value of information to the point where George Gilder asserts that in the past 15 years, the useful life of worker skills and knowledge has declined from 7 to 14 years to 3 to 5 years.

He further suggests that we are at the end of the age of the specialist as we know it. Specialists have traditionally been people who knew more and more about less and less, narrowing their focus as they went. Now we are entering the time of the momentary specialist. A momentary specialist is someone, who, while maintaining a narrow focus, also has the ability to access, organize, and apply new information as it appears. For momentary specialists, their particular expertise may be constantly or suddenly changing. For them, the starting point is their information-processing skills, which are the basis of their ability to regularly shift their area of expertise in an information-driven society. For the momentary specialist, it's no longer just about being an expert in a static field. Rather, it's about having the ability to deal effectively with a constantly changing world.

What's the Cure for IDD?

To effectively manage information requires a completely different set of skills than those that were needed in the past. Successfully navigating through vast quantities of information of varying quality requires the ability to ask the right questions; access the data sources; synthesize, analyze, and authenticate the information; and apply what has been developed to provide solutions to real problems.

The starting point for dealing with IDD is to acknowledge that things have changed irrevocably in the past few years. We live in a very different world that requires us to get beyond TTWWADI (that's the way we've always done it). It's time for all of us to learn a new set of core skills that will help us to stay afloat and ride the wave of change of the Information Age.

What Is InfoSavvy?

Repeated practice with information literacy skills leads one to become information-ally fluent. This is what we call InfoSavvy. Being InfoSavvy means that the more you practice information-processing skills, the more they become a natural aspect of everyday thinking. When we drive a car or read a book, all of our learned skills are used intuitively. In the same way, when InfoSavvy skills are learned and repeatedly practiced, they become an intuitive, integrated whole. Being InfoSavvy moves the focus from the conscious consideration of the skills to the transparent application of the skills to solve any information need or problem.

The Changing Face of Literacy

When public education first became widespread in the 1800s, being "literate" meant having the knowledge to read and write. In the 1900s, being literate expanded to being "well-read"—being knowledgeable about a variety of cultural subjects, such as art, literature, and the classics.

In the 2000s, as the Information Age increasingly comes to dominate our lives, the meaning of being literate is expanding again to include a wide range of knowledge management techniques. In the Information Age "information literacy" requires strong critical thinking skills, which is the ability to process data into knowledge through creative analyzing, synthesizing, and problem solving. Good listening and speaking skills are also becoming essential since collaborating with others and working in teams is more important than ever before. In addition, our established knowledge base is being superseded by new knowledge at an astonishing rate. This trend is leading to diminishing the value of older, fact-based knowledge, while at the same time increasing the value of the skills required to process new information effectively.

Success in Industrial Age schools and factories was based primarily on knowing facts. But in a rapidly changing world, facts can soon become irrelevant, outdated, or just plain wrong. An education based only on facts no longer has any permanent value. In the Information Age, it's essential to spend more time teaching children information-processing skills and less time teaching rote memorization and repetition. This new emphasis on the importance of information-processing skills is at the heart of InfoSavvy.

This book is designed to help students develop the information literacy skills that are needed for success in the Information Age.

Chapter 3

Understanding InfoSavvy
and NetSavvy

The Effect of New Technologies on Today's Workplace

Today's high-tech and knowledge-based industries require not just people who can read or who are well read, but people who can use their reading skills to process information in all its current forms. Literacy in this fast-changing world is less about "What knowledge did you acquire years ago in school?" and more about "What can you do with the knowledge available today?" With the huge increase in the amount of available information, it's no longer about "How many information sources can you access?" as much as it's about "Can you sift through the myriad of sources to find the most relevant and reliable ones?" or "Can you find or create the information that we need to solve a specific problem right now?"

This is a remarkable change from what employers required from the average clerical or industrial worker not long ago. Workers were placed in a rigid hierarchy and expected to be punctual, to quietly follow orders, and to do things without question. Workers would have acquired most of the knowledge necessary for a good job by the time they had finished school or a training program. For a long time, a specialized knowledge base could get you a reasonable, well-paid career for life in a factory or an office. Then suddenly, things changed.

The emergence of the Information Age and the increasing power of information systems combined with rapid advances in communication systems caused widespread downsizing in the traditional Industrial Age workforce, including the elimination of whole sectors of the economy. Today, the fastest growing sectors of the economy are those associated with the information-based, high-technology and communications industries.

The Heart of Being InfoSavvy

Unfortunately, many of today's students are not being adequately prepared for the Information Age. It's so new and changing so rapidly that many others have not been formally prepared for it either, including parents, professionals, business executives, or even teachers. The purpose of InfoSavvy is to help teachers systematically provide information literacy experiences for students at all grade levels and in all subject areas. The key process that InfoSavvy uses for any information-processing task is known as the **five aspects (5As) of information literacy**, and this is at the heart of how to become InfoSavvy.

The 5As of Information Literacy

There are five basic steps that can be used to solve any information need:

1. *Asking* (key questions to be answered)
2. *Accessing* (relevant information)
3. *Analyzing* (the acquired information)
4. *Applying* (the information to a task)
5. *Assessing* (the end result and the process)

The Jean-Luc Picard Approach to Solving Problems

To illustrate how the 5As can deal with actual information needs, let's begin by zooming ahead at warp speed and spending a day with Jean-Luc Picard, captain of the starship *Enterprise*. He has the complex job of dealing with the vast cultural differences among the crew, not to mention the technical responsibilities of running a starship, and the apparently ongoing task of avoiding intergalactic war. He also needs to constantly manage huge amounts of information to solve a host of every-day problems and needs. Let's consider how he goes about handling the challenges of daily life.

Obviously he isn't able to hold all of the necessary information in his head. What does he do? He relies on his crew, as well as on a vast network of information technologies (ITs) and a massive information database—what we call the Internet today—to solve his problems. He uses the simple, five-step process described above to solve any number of problems that come his way. The 5As of the InfoSavvy model that he uses are as follows.

- *Asking:* Aware that there's an information need, he considers its context. He then develops a series of problem-related questions to ask of himself, the crew, and the information systems.
- *Accessing:* Based on the questions he has created, he uses a variety of information resources and tools to gather as much data about the information need as he can.
- *Analyzing:* He examines the data and begins to turn it into knowledge by checking its usefulness, suitability, and authenticity.
- *Applying:* It's time to take action! He attempts to solve the problem by assembling the various pieces he has analyzed and then applies the knowledge gained to identify the aliens, avert intergalactic war, save the galaxy, or find a parking spot.

- *Assessing:* Late at night, alone in his quarters, Picard sits with the Captain's Log, reflects on the events that have taken place, assesses the processes that were used, and evaluates the results.

The 5As Approach

This five-stage InfoSavvy process allows him to filter the background noise of InfoWhelm. Filtering provides relevance and context for the effective use of information. Let's now examine each of these five steps more carefully to see what makes Jean-Luc so InfoSavvy.

1. Asking

Asking requires the ability to clearly define the problem and its context in terms of questions. In asking the right questions, Picard sets boundaries and defines the initial parameters for his research, determining what needs to be done to solve the problem. This gives a context and relevance to the mission and helps him make the right connections. It's in the process of addressing these questions that Captain Picard gains ownership of the learning, as well as responsibility for the data.

Crucial Asking skills include

- Understanding the problem to be solved
- Identifying key words and forming questions around them
- Brainstorming
- Thinking laterally
- Understanding ethical issues
- Listening deeply, viewing wisely, and speaking critically
- Filtering information white noise
- Sharing personal knowledge and experience

2. Accessing

Accessing is the wild card of the information cycle because at this stage, the pathways to be followed are totally speculative. One thing tends to lead to another, which means that just about anything can happen. *Accessing* requires Jean-Luc to make links between various data. Through experience, he has learned how to effectively distinguish what should be kept from what should be discarded.

It's important to note that the techniques and skills he uses here are media independent. The various techniques are equally effective whether they are used with a book, a computer, a microfiche, a video, or the Internet. In consciously moving away from a single text or medium as the information resource of choice, the *Accessing* strategies become more important than the specific tools being used. Thus, the choice of tool is largely determined by the information need.

Crucial Accessing skills include

- Determining where the information is
- Determining what skills are needed to find it
- Using a variety of paper and electronic sources
- Prioritizing searching strategies
- Skimming, scanning, and scouring resources for pertinent data
- Doing simple research
- Using filtering skills
- Taking smart notes

3. Analyzing

Analyzing is where the "aha"! experience is created as the different pieces of data are put together. Effective analysis requires that Jean-Luc be able to look at the data critically to see the patterns as they emerge. This includes the ability to identify missing information, to deal with incomplete information, to separate facts from opinions, and to establish the authenticity and credibility of the data. Doing this allows Jean-Luc to turn the data into usable information. The *Analyzing* stage is not a linear process as it may require him to repeatedly revisit his original questions and to access additional data to address the information need more precisely.

Crucial Analyzing skills include

- Organizing and summarizing data from a variety of sources
- Working independently and collaboratively with peers, teachers, or other individuals to document the authenticity and analysis of the data
- Checking data for relevance
- Listing and distinguishing between good, bad, and ugly data sources
- Differentiating fact from opinion
- Examining data for underlying meaning and bias
- Determining when the data answer the original questions and identifying when there is incomplete information
- Revisiting the Asking or Accessing stages to fill in the blanks
- Documenting, crediting, and taking notes to determine authenticity
- Using probability, trends, and best guesses to seek out additional data as needed
- Using all of the above skills to turn the data into useful information

4. Applying

At the application stage, Jean-Luc uses the data that have been accessed, analyzed, and turned into knowledge to take action. In the InfoSavvy context, this knowledge would be used to solve a problem, write an essay, develop a report, create a graph, complete an argument, make a presentation, or do whatever else needs to be done.

At this stage, Picard is dealing with various combinations of the four flavors of information: text, video, audio, and images. The flavors can be assembled in a variety of ways. For Jean-Luc, the critical skill at this stage is being able to take what he's got and address the issue. *Applying* is the stage where products are created, actions are taken, problems are solved, or information needs are satisfied. Being able to access huge amounts of data means nothing unless the data are effectively analyzed, turned into personal knowledge, *and* then applied to resolving the issue.

Crucial Applying skills include

- Identifying an appropriate format for presenting the information
- Applying the format to present the information or solution to the problem

5.   Assessing

The *Assessing* stage is the reflective, soul-searching part of the process. Alone in his quarters, Picard revisits each stage of the process and reflects upon the pathways that he followed to get from raw data to information and knowledge. At this stage, he wants to consider not just what was learned, but how it was learned. What worked? What didn't? How could the product, process, or solution have been improved? What could be done better the next time around?

Crucial Assessing skills include

- Asking questions about the processes used and the information obtained
- Reflecting critically on the process
- Acting on these reflections
- Internalizing new learnings
- Transferring the learning to other situations

Becoming InfoSavvy

Regular use of the five stages of the InfoSavvy process has led Jean-Luc to a higher level of information literacy. In fact, Picard has gone beyond being information *literate* to being information *fluent*. Through repeated practice, the individual steps have become transparent, blended in to a single process. The Captain no longer pauses to consider each step separately. Rather he continuously applies them to intuitively solve everyday problems. The process he uses is a spiraling hierarchy of continuous As. *Asking* leads to *Accessing*. *Accessing* leads to *Analyzing*. *Analyzing* leads to *Applying*. *Applying* leads to *Assessing*, which then leads back to a new level of *Asking*.

Becoming NetSavvy

To this point, we have focused on the 5As of InfoSavvy. This process is the basis for solving virtually any information need. Now we will address the issues of information literacy as they apply to using the Internet to solve an information need. This is the specific subset of InfoSavvy skills needed to become Internet literate or NetSavvy.

The Internet is a unique resource—a three-in-one grab bag of tools unlike any other resources we've ever experienced. It's a communications tool, a research tool, and a publication tool. To be NetSavvy is simply to use specific InfoSavvy skills as they apply to these three aspects of the Internet. Information fluency in all media is to be InfoSavvy, and information fluency as it applies to the Internet is to be NetSavvy.

What Isn't NetSavvy?

Someone suffering from InfoWhelm or at the early stages of technological awareness may assume that buying a computer and learning how to navigate the Internet using a technical manual is the whole solution. Successful learning encompasses much more than this. NetSavvy is not about the decontexualized use of Internet software tools or information-processing skills taught in isolation. From a NetSavvy perspective, the best way to learn about the Internet is to use a Web browser, an e-mail program, or a search engine as a tool to solve a personal need. Deep learning happens only when you use the hardware and software in the context of solving a specific problem. Learning about the hardware and software tools is only a by-product of that problem-solving process.

Now let's turn our attention to how NetSavvy skills can be successfully implemented in the classroom and how the full potential of the Internet can be realized. In Part II, we introduce the reader to the details of the NetSavvy process, including the Teacher Lesson Planners and the Student Tools that work with the NetSavvy Skills Framework. Read on!

Part II

Setting up the NetSavvy Classroom

Getting Started

The idea of NetSavvy is for students to learn information-processing skills while completing relevant student projects in almost any subject area, from physical education (PE) to mathematics to English to home economics, and at any grade level. The NetSavvy skills are designed to be embedded into the learning cycle to maximize the possibilities for research and presentation, rather than being introduced as a separate subject. There are three elements to the NetSavvy process. These are the Teacher Lesson Planners, the Student Tools, and the Skills Framework.

The Teacher Lesson Planners are designed to allow teachers to work closely with the Skills Framework to quickly develop lesson plans using the 5As process to integrate information literacy skills into project-based learning. The Student Tools systematically guide the student through each stage of the 5As process. The Skills Framework is a comprehensive and structured compilation of many of the skills needed to become information literate using the Internet as a resource.

The NetSavvy Tools and Framework at a Glance

The starting point of the NetSavvy process occurs when a teacher first considers doing a project. The Ten-Minute Lesson Planner can be used to quickly identify which of the NetSavvy Skill Sets the teacher wants to introduce or extend in conjunction with the project. The Ten-Minute Lesson Planner is followed by five separate chapters, one for each stage of the NetSavvy 5As process. Each chapter is structured in the same manner. First, the Lesson Planner for that A is introduced along with a worked example of how the tool can be used. Each Lesson Planner is aligned with the Skills Framework to guide the teacher through the project-planning process. At each stage, the prerequisite skills, the possible instructional methods, the equipment needs, the information literacy skills to be introduced or reinforced, and the assessment strategies are considered. Finally the Student Tools that guide the student to each stage of the 5As process are introduced. All the tools are shown as worked examples to demonstrate how they may be used. Figure II.1 represents all the NetSavvy tools and elements and how they work together.

Figure II.1. How the NetSavvy Tools and Elements Work Together

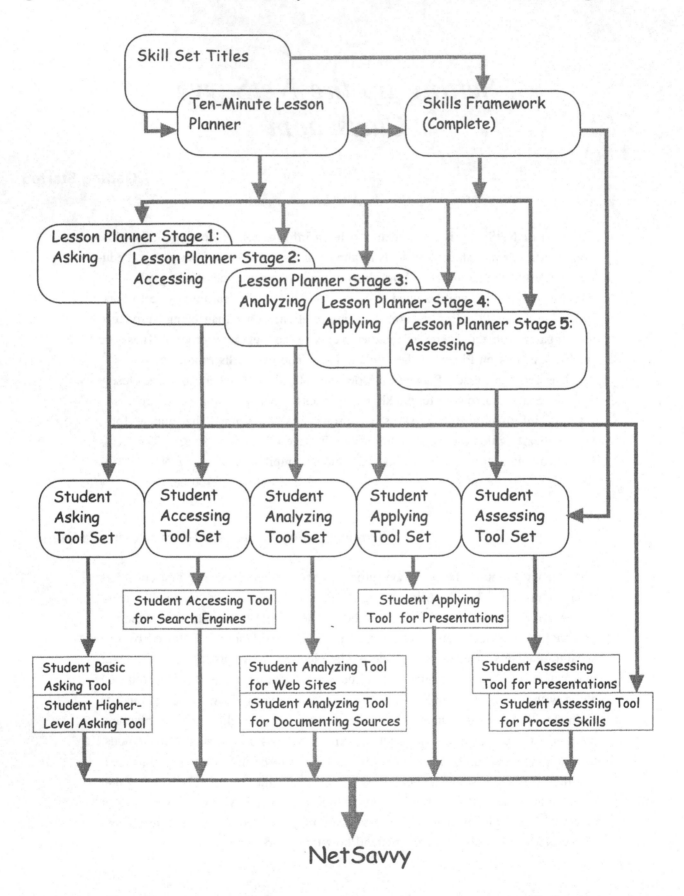

A Quick Review of the 5As of Information Literacy

The NetSavvy 5As process is the basis of completing almost any task. The five basic stages for solving any information need are

1. *Asking* (key questions to be answered)
2. *Accessing* (relevant data)
3. *Analyzing* (the acquired data)
4. *Applying* (the data to the task)
5. *Assessing* (both the end result and the process)

Summary of the Uses of the NetSavvy Framework

The NetSavvy Framework serves many purposes. First, the Framework provides a comprehensive organized list of information literacy skills as they pertain to the Internet. Second, the Framework can be used to determine what prerequisite Skill Sets students need to have to complete a project. A Skill Set consists of a group of related skills that collectively help a teacher to teach a major information literacy competency. Third, the Framework can be used as a checklist to assess the specific information literacy skills that a student may already have and the extent to which these skills have been mastered. Finally, the Framework can be used to identify specific skills that the teacher wants to introduce or reinforce as an integrated element of the project. The Skills Framework outlines the thinking skills relevant to each stage of the 5As process and the information-processing and technological skills that can assist in implementing them. Each of the 5As stage in the Skills Framework is organized into five sections in the following manner:

1. *Asking* Skills
   A. *Asking* Essential Skill sets
   B. *Asking* Prerequisite Skill sets
   C. *Asking* Techniques Skill sets
   D. *Asking* Technology Skill sets
   E. *Asking* Review Skill sets

2. *Accessing* Skills
   A. *Accessing* Essential Skill sets
   B. *Accessing* Prerequisite Skill sets
   C. *Accessing* Techniques Skill sets
   D. *Accessing* Technology Skill sets
   E. *Accessing* Review Skill sets

3. . . . and so on

The five sections of each stage of the 5As process can be visualized as pieces of a puzzle. These are the Essential, Prerequisite, Techniques, Technology, and Review aspects of NetSavvy for each A. When taught together as an integrated whole, they complete the puzzle and create the "whole picture" of that stage. Figure II.2 shows how the five pieces fit together.

The "Essential Skills" component represents the core or critical skills that must be taught to master that A. The "Prerequisite Skills" element consists of the foundational skills that must already be in place to help students learn the more advanced

Figure II.2. Fitting the NetSavvy Pieces Together

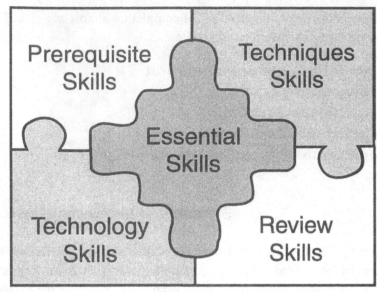

essential skills. The "Techniques Skills" describe methods that may be used to learn new skills for that stage. The "Technology Skills" include hardware and software skills that can assist students in learning or reinforcing new skills. Finally, the "Reviewing Skills" are the set of skills that help students assess and reflect upon their learning of that A.

In the next chapter (Chapter 4), we introduce the first NetSavvy lesson planning tool for teachers, entitled the "Ten-Minute Lesson Planner," along with a summary of the Skills Framework Skill Sets (Figure 4.1). In subsequent chapters (Chapters 5 through 9), we present specific lesson planning tools and student tools for each A of the five stages. In addition to the overview of all the tools and how they work together provided in Figure II.1, the complete Skills Framework is provided in Part III together with blank copies of all the teacher and student tools in Appendixes A and B, respectively.

How We Introduce the Tools

To demonstrate how all the tools can be applied, we use the thinking and planning of Ms. Penny Jones, a 6th-grade teacher, who decides to develop a project on whales using the Internet as a major resource. The worked examples of the teacher tools have been done by Ms. Jones, whereas the worked examples of the student tools have been completed by Jessica Pembroke, a student in Ms. Jones's class. Jessica is working with a group of students who have formed a team based on a common interest in beluga whales.

Chapter 4

Introducing the Ten-Minute Lesson Planner

What Is the Ten-Minute Lesson Planner?

The NetSavvy Ten-Minute Lesson Planner (Figure 4.2) is used as a preliminary planning tool by the teacher. The purpose of the tool is to help integrate curricular content with process skills quickly and efficiently. The tool helps the teacher to create an overview of the content being covered, the NetSavvy Skill Sets of the 5As to be addressed, the curriculum connections and real world connections to be made, and the assessment of content and process skills. Figure 4.1 is a summary of the Skills Framework Skill Sets (a Skill Set consists of a group of related skills that collectively help a teacher to teach a major information literacy competency). Its purpose is to provide a quick reference to the main competencies or Skill Sets of NetSavvy. The Ten-Minute Lesson Planner shown in Figure 4.2 includes instructions, tips, and suggestions for using the tool effectively. A blank version of the tool is provided in Appendix A to be photocopied and enlarged if so required. The Ten-Minute Lesson Planner is made up of seven major components, which are as follows:

1. *Asking*—directs the teacher to identify resources for introducing the topic in a manner that will optimize student interest and responsibility for learning, as well as what prerequisite skills will be needed by students to successfully complete this stage of the process

2. *Accessing*—helps teachers to identify which resources they want students to use to access data for researching a topic, as well as what prerequisite skills will be needed by students to successfully complete this stage of the process

3. *Analyzing*—helps the teacher to consider the methods that students could or should use to study, document, and authenticate the sources of data that students will access, as well as what prerequisite skills will be needed by students to successfully complete this stage of the process

4. *Applying*—asks the teacher to consider what form student presentation/products will be in, as well as what prerequisite skills will be needed by students to successfully complete this stage of the process

5. *Assessing*—the central part of the tool, helps the teacher to think through which aspects of the content and process skills will be assessed and how this will be done, as well as what prerequisite skills will be needed by students to successfully complete this stage of the process

Figure 4.1a: NetSavvy Framework Skill Set Titles for Stages 1, 2 & 3

Stage 1: *ASKING*

1A. *Asking* Essential Skill Sets
1. Critical Conversing Skill Set—Observing & Questioning
2. Critical Conversing Skill Set—Listening & Questioning
3. Critical Conversing Skill Set—Thinking & Questioning

1B. *Asking* Prerequisite Skill Sets
1. General Observing Skill Set
2. General Listening Skill Set
3. General Speaking Skill Set

1C. *Asking* Techniques Skill Sets
1. Brainstorming Skill Set
2. Question Forming Skill Set
3. General Conversing Skill Set
4. Critical Conversing Skill Set

1D. *Asking* Technology Skill Sets
1. Computer Software Skill Set
2. Computer Hardware Skill Set

1E. *Asking* Review Skill Sets
1. Student Process Review Skill Set
2. Collaborative Process Review Skill Set
3. Teacher Process Review

Stage 2: *ACCESSING*

2A. *Accessing* Essential Skill Sets
1. Skill Set for Using Hardware
2. Skill Set for Using Computer Software

2B. *Accessing* Prerequisite Skill Sets
1. General Workstation Skill Set
2. General Computer Skill Set
3. General Internet Skill Set
4. Internet On-line Skill Set
5. General Reading Skill Set
6. Technical Reading Skill Set

2C. *Accessing* Techniques Skill Sets
1. Starting Point Skill Set
2. Considering Internet Indexing Systems
3. Considering Data Sources by Location
4. Considering Internet Tools for Locating People
5. Considering Possible Internet Tools for Interacting
   with People in Real Time
6. Considering Accessing Peoples' Original Internet Data
7. Considering Accessing Peoples' Interpreted Internet Data
8. Considering Traditional Sources Skill Set
9. Considering Contemplative Thinking Skill Set

2D. *Accessing* Technology Skill Sets
1. Considering Other Software for Accessing Data
2. Considering Possible Hardware for Accessing Data

2E. *Accessing* Review Skill Sets
1. Student Process Review Skill Set
2. Collaborative Process Review Skill Set
3. Teacher Process Review

Stage 3: *ANALYZING*

3A. *Analyzing* Essential Skill Sets
1. General Analyzing Skill Set
2. Critical Analyzing Skill Set
3. Media Analyzing Skill Set
4. General Documenting Skill Set
5. Documenting Skill Set—Internet
6. Critical Authenticating Skill Set

3B. *Analyzing* Prerequisite Skill Sets
1. General Thinking Skill Set
2. Critical Thinking Skill Set

3C. *Analyzing* Techniques Skill Sets
1. Considering Methods for Analyzing Data

3D. *Analyzing* Technology Skill Sets
1. Considering Computer Software for Analyzing Data
2. Considering Computer Hardware for Analyzing Data

3E. *Analyzing* Review Skill Sets
1. Student Process Review Skill Set
2. Collaborative Process Review Skill Set

Figure 4.1b: NetSavvy Framework Skill Set Titles for Stages 4 & 5

Stage 4: *APPLYING*

4A. *Applying* Essential Skill Sets
1. Skill Set for Preparing Materials from Several Sources
2. General Presentation Skill Set
3. Graphics Presentation Skill Set
4. Writing Presentation Skill Set
5. Technical Writing Presentation Skill Set
6. Oral Presentation Skill Set
7. Debating Skill Set
8. Audio Presentation Skill Set
9. Video Presentation Skill Set
10. Multimedia Presentation Skill Set
11. Internet Publishing Presentation Skill Set
12. General—Finalizing the Preparation of a Presentation

4B. *Applying* Prerequisite Skill Sets
1. Basic Skill Set for Preparation of a Presentation
2. General Presentation Skill Set Using Graphics
3. General Presentation Skill Set Using Writing
4. General Technical Writing Presentation Skill Set
5. General Audio Presentation Skill Set
6. General Video Presentation Skill Set
7. General Multimedia Presentation Skill Set
8. General—Consults with a Teacher or Peers

4C. *Applying* Techniques Skill Sets
1. General Considerations
2. Graphics
3. Writing
4. Technical Writing
5. Oral Presentation
6. Debate
7. Audio Presentation
8. Video Presentation
9. Multimedia Presentation
10. Internet Publishing

4D. *Applying* Technology Skill Sets
1. Using Hardware
2. Using Computer Software

4E. *Applying* Review Skill Sets
1. Student Self-Assessment Questionnaire
2. Collaborative Process Review Skill Set

Stage 5: *ASSESSING*

5A. *Assessing* Essential Skill Sets
1. Presentation Self-Assessment Questionnaire
2. Technique Assessment Questionnaire
3. Technology Assessment Questionnaire
4. Process Assessment Questionnaire
5. Transfer of Learning

5B. *Assessing* Prerequisite Skill Sets
1. Starting Point Skill Set

5C. *Assessing* Techniques Skill Sets
1. Considering Presentation Assessing Methods
2. Considering Process Assessing Methods

5D. *Assessing* Technology Skill Sets
1. Presentation Assessing Tools
2. Process Assessing Tools

5E. *Assessing* Review Skill Sets
1. Teacher Review of Assessing
2. Project Review by Others

Figure 4.2. Ten-Minute Lesson Planner:
Instructions, Tips and Suggestions for Use

1. ASKING (Framework, 1C Skill Sets)

Consider techniques for introducing the topic that will optimize student interest and responsibility for learning. These might include brainstorming, books, stories, students' personal experiences, experts, movies, other teachers...

Prerequisites (Framework, 1B Skill Sets)

Make a note to check that your students have the basic Asking skills you assume they have.

2. ACCESSING (Framework, 2C Skill Sets)

What techniques do you want students to use to access data for researching the topic? These might include paper-based sources, the Internet, CD-ROMs, interviewing people and the student Accessing tool.

Prerequisites (Framework, 2B Skill Sets)

Make a note to check that your students have the basic Accessing skills you assume they'll need to do the work.

Content

What are your content objectives? Do you want students to focus on specific areas of interest, or do all students have to learn the same content? Is the content relevant to your students? How can you make it relevant? Does the content have a broad enough focus so that it connects to the students' real world, their social world, or the real world of work? Are there philosophical, moral and/or aesthetic issues in the content that could/should be considered?

Prerequisite content knowledge

Make a note to check that your students have knowledge of the basic content you assume they should already have to do the work.

5. ASSESSING

Content to be assessed
Consider what content you want to assess, and what content you want to have students or others assess.

Process skills to be assessed (Framework, 5A Skill Sets)
Use the skills targeted in all 5 of the Teacher Lesson Planners to create a Student Assessing Tool for Process skills.

Prerequisites (Framework, 5B Skill Sets)

Check the Skills Framework (5B) to identify the basic skills students should have so that they can reflect on and assess the learning experiences and processes they have gone through.

Connections

Curriculum
Consider the 5As information literacy skills and the content that you are planning to have students learn. Do the content areas and process skills connect with other areas of the curriculum such as Math, Language Arts, PE, Science, Art and so on? The more connections the better.

Outside school

Outside school connections are also termed as "global connections." How can you help students to make global connections which encompass all aspects of life—social, work, professional, ethical, moral...

3. ANALYZING (Framework, 3C Skill Sets)

Consider the techniques students should use to study, document and authenticate the sources of data accessed. These might include outlines, webs, databases, quotes, bibliographic references and using the student Analzying tools.

Prerequisites (Framework, 3B Skill Sets)

Make a note to check that your students have the basic Analyzing skills you assume they'll need to do the work.

4. APPLYING (Framework, 4C Skill Sets)

Consider what form student presentations will be in:

Paper-Based	Computer	Other
report	writing	oral
speech	drawing	audio
display	multimedia	video

Prerequisites (Framework, 4B Skill Sets)

Make a note to check that your students have the basic Applying skills you assume they'll need to do the work.

6. *Content*—asks the teacher to consider the content objectives, as well as the prerequisite content knowledge that will be needed to make the learning of new content easier

7. *Connections*—asks the teacher to consider connections of both content and process skills to other areas of the curriculum and to the world outside of school

In our worked example, the Ten-Minute Lesson Planner is used to plan a 6th-grade project on whales (Figure 4.3). However, the same tool can be used at any grade level and in any area of the curriculum. The tool is used together with the summary of Skills Framework Skill Set titles. A Skill Set consists of a group of related skills that are used collectively to help the teacher introduce a major information literacy competency. The summary of Skills Framework Skill Sets is an abbreviated version of the whole Skills Framework, which lists all the Framework's headings or names of the Skill Sets and all the individual skills belonging to that Set. Using a summary rather than the entire Framework makes this stage of the planning quick and easy to do.

In this example, Ms. Jones has used the Ten-Minute Planner to organize the many details she feels are essential to the success of the project. However, different teachers will use the Planner in a variety of ways, entering as much or as little detail as needed.

How Ms. Jones Uses the Ten-Minute Lesson Planner

Penny Jones decides to do a project on whales with her 6th-grade class. After first referring to the Science Curriculum Guide to help her decide what her content objectives are, she fills in the *Content* section of the Ten-Minute Planner. Next, to get a quick overview of the skills involved in this particular project, she checks the Skills Framework Skill Set summary shown in Figure 4.1. The abbreviated version of the complete Skills Framework, which lists all the Framework's headings (Skill Sets) is scanned for ideas to fill in the boxes labeled with the stages of the 5As process from Stage 1 *Asking* to Stage 5 *Assessing*. For each of the five stages, Ms. Jones also knows that there are student tools that guide students through the *Asking, Accessing, Analyzing, Applying,* and *Assessing* stages of the project and will use them as and when needed.

As Ms. Jones makes notes about how to introduce the subject of whales, she considers different strategies she can use to engage students in generating questions, as well as ways to get them to share their knowledge and experiences on the topic. She fills in the *Asking* section of the Ten-Minute Planner with her ideas.

Having filled out the *Asking* section, she moves on to the *Accessing* section of the Planner, where she brainstorms how her students will access the data for a project on whales. Although she intends to use Internet search engines primarily to locate relevant Web sites about whales on the Internet, she also considers other possible electronic and paper-based resources.

Once the *Accessing* section is complete, she moves on to *Analyzing*. Here, she decides how students will analyze, authenticate, and document their sources of

Figure 4.3. Ten-Minute Lesson Planner:
Example by Ms. Jones for her Grade 6 "Whales" Project

1. ASKING (Framework, 1C Skill Sets)

- information for class brainstorming session from aquarium Web sites; whale-watching brochure; movie Free Willy; personal experiences; textbooks; CD-ROMs; newspapers; magazines; local experts.

1C1 Brainstorming Skill Set

Prerequisites (Framework, 1B Skill Sets)
- class has done this before so this not an issue

2. ACCESSING (Framework, 2C Skill Sets)

- learn to use Internet search engines for research
- consult group members and others (parents) to find other resources eg. Newspapers, books, CD-ROMs for deeper focus on special interest issues.

2C2 Consider Internet Indexing Systems

Prerequisites (Framework, 2B Skill Sets)
- establish level of experience with search engines

Content

- classification of whales
- differences between whales and other animals
- physical characteristics
- whale sizes compared to other animals
- life cycle, reproduction, care of young
- social behavior
- geographic distribution, habitat
- feeding habits
- environmental issues - whale hunting
- whale watching
- choose a specific group of whales per group for deeper focused study (optional)

Prerequisite content knowledge
- know the differences between mammals, fish, amphibians & reptiles

5. ASSESSING
Content to be assessed
- 1000 word report
- mark out of 100 with comments
- classification of whales
- physical characteristics
- life cycle, reproduction, care of young
- geographic distribution, habitat
- feeding habits
- method of Assessing: see 5C

Process skills to be assessed (Framework, 5C Skill Sets)

- Will make a Student Assessing Tool for Process Skills based on details from the 5 Lesson Planners
- Use Student Assessing Tool for Presentations as is

Prerequisites (Framework, 5B Skill Sets)
5B1 Starting point skill set

Connections
Curriculum

- Language Arts: making notes, writing reports, improving research skills
- Science: scientific facts about whales, improving research skills
- Math: comparison of whale sizes with other objects and animals, estimation & comparison
- other: learning to work collaboratively, listening

Outside school
- improving writing skills
- introducing report writing, expository writing skills
- improving verbal communication by working collaboratively in a team
- reinforcing listening skills
- raising level of environmental awareness
- raising ethical issues around whale hunting

3. ANALYZING (Framework, 3C Skill Sets)

Use Student Analyzing Tool for Documenting Sources and Student Analyzing Tool for Web Sites in conjunction with the Student Accessing Tool for Search Engines

Prerequisites (Framework, 3B Skill Sets)
check how students were taught to document sources

4. APPLYING (Framework, 4C Skill Sets)

Consider what form student presentations will be in:

Paper-Based	Computer	Other	
(report)	(writing)	oral	- 1000 word report
speech	drawing	audio	
display	multimedia	video	

Prerequisites (Framework, 4B Skill Sets)
4B3 Check Skill Set for writing.

data—in this case, Web sites and their authors. Moving on, in the *Applying* section she firms up the details of how students will be expected to present (apply) their information. For this whale project, Ms. Jones opts for a form of presentation her students are familiar with, a report done with a word processor containing some illustrations.

Next, in the *Assessing* section of the Ten-Minute Planner, she decides what aspects of the content will be tested and how this will be done. Since much of what students learned on the project will have involved the development of process skills, she considers how these can also be assessed.

Finally, looking back over the proposed project, Ms. Jones considers how the content and processes learned will connect with the curriculum in other subject area, as well as how this project may have relevance to students' life outside of school. She fills in the section titled *Connections*.

It is important to note that whereas, in this example, the Ten-Minute Lesson Planner was introduced in a linear manner, there is no set or specific way of working the tool—it is designed so that a teacher can start anywhere and work in any direction. How Ms. Jones decided to use the tool represents only one approach.

In Summary

The Ten-Minute Lesson Planner offers a quick way to brainstorm NetSavvy lesson plans. The primary purpose of the Planner is to help ensure that, over time, all the criteria for learning information literacy skills are addressed. This includes both content and process skills. The secondary focus of the Planner is to encourage the embedding of information literacy skills within all instructional units and into all aspects of lesson planning—from single lessons to major projects and thematic units. The Ten-Minute Lesson Planner template can be found in Appendix A.

In the following five chapters, Chapter 5 through 9, we will present teacher Lesson Planners for each of the five stages of the NetSavvy process. This is where much more detailed lesson planning can be done. With these planning tools, Ms. Jones can now select specific skills from the previously identified Skill Sets that she wishes to introduce or reinforce. Read on!

Chapter 5

Stage 1: ASKING—Teacher and Student Tools

In this chapter we introduce three tools: the Stage 1: *Asking* Lesson Planner (Figure 5.1) for teachers, the Student Basic *Asking* Tool (Figure 5.2), and the Student Higher-Level *Asking* Tool (Figure 5.3). All three tools are presented as worked examples. Blank versions of these tools that can be photocopied for use are found in Appendixes A and B.

Note: When a teacher is introducing an assignment, the details of what the students are to produce and how they will be assessed on their work can be clarified using the *Applying* Tool and the two *Assessing* Tools. The first parts of the *Applying* Tool and the *Assessing* Tool for Presentations are designed to be used at the beginning of a project as a way of engaging students in the *Applying* and *Assessing* processes and developing student input. When the *Assessing* Tool for Process Skills is introduced at the beginning of the project, it serves to assess the student's current skill levels. Once the project is completed, this same tool can be given back to the students so that they can reassess their levels of understanding. This provides both the student and the teacher with a snapshot of how much learning has actually occurred during the project as well as what still needs to be improved.

Stage 1: *Asking* Lesson Planner

The Stage 1: *Asking* Lesson Planner, shown in Figure 5.1, is used with the Ten-Minute Lesson Planner described in Chapter 4. The purpose of the *Asking* Lesson Planner is to help the teacher plan the integration of specific *Asking* stage skills into the objectives of any instructional unit or project. The *Asking* Lesson Planner is a detailed extension of the *Asking* component of the Ten-Minute Lesson Planner, where the teacher identified general *Asking* Skill Sets to be addressed during the project. Using the *Asking* Lesson Planner, the teacher identifies the specific *Asking* skills to be introduced and/or reinforced. These skills are organized under the *Asking* Skill Sets of the complete Skills Framework, which is located in Part III.

Figure 5.1 shows a completed version of Ms. Jones's lesson plan for implementing the *Asking* stage. The Stage 1: *Asking* Lesson Planner is structured in exactly the same way as the lesson planners for *Accessing, Analyzing, Applying,* and *Assessing.* The *Asking* Lesson Planner has five components, which are designed to work with the five major components of the *Asking* Skills Framework. Structurally, each of the components in the Planner outlines the goal of the component, gives a summary of the skill sets in that component, and lists the sections related to planning the implementation of that component. Figure 5.1 shows how Ms. Jones has used this tool.

Figure 5.1. Stage 1: ASKING Lesson Planner

1B. Asking **Prerequisite Skills**

Goal: to check your assumptions about what basic Asking skills students must already have

Basic Student Skills Needed

(1. Observing) (2. Listening) (3. Speaking)

- 1B1 General Observing Skill Set - check verbally for problems
- 1B2 General Listening Skill Set - check verbally for problems and check who has done idea mapping before
- 1B3 General Speaking Skill Set - have students see me privately

Add any basic skills that are not included in the Skills Framework to the Essential Skills section below

1C. Asking **Techniques Skills**

Goal: to engage students in this topic by stimulating their interest to discuss the topic and ask questions

Possible Methods

(Student Basic Asking Tool)
Student Higher-Level Asking Tool

(1. Brainstorming)   (2. Question Forming)
3. General Conversing   4. Critical Conversing

- brainstorm using idea maps
- science text reading
- movie Free Willy
- whale stories

1A. Asking **Essential Skills**

Goal: to identify the question-asking and conversing skills you want students to develop during the Asking stage of the project

(1. Observing & Questioning)   2. Listening & Questioning   (3. Thinking & Questioning)

Skills to be introduced

- 1C1(a) Creates idea maps
- 1B1(a) See me privately about problems
- 1A3(b) Uses personal interpretations of experiences, stories, poems, plays or movies to generate questions

Skills to be reinforced

- 1A3(a) Asks questions which focus on new areas of knowledge and application
- 1A3(e) Asks hypothetical questions of experiences for exploring possibilities and testing relationships

1D. Asking **Equipment Needs**

Goal: to ensure that the equipment needed to do the Asking stage is available and working properly

1. **Software needs**   2. **Hardware needs**
(a. Word processor)   (a. Computer)
- use MS Word   - use library computer
(b. Search engine)   b. Other
- use AltaVista
c. Idea and concept mapping

d. CD-Rom

(e. Other)
- have students use paper and pencils to practice idea and concept mapping

1E. Asking **Review Skills**

Goal: to check that the Asking stage processes are properly and fully implemented

1. **Student Process Review**

- none

2. (**Collaborative Process Review**)

- 1E2(a) Works with others to review process by comparing progress to date with initial goals

3. **Teacher Process Review**

- Do class review using the Asking Tool results

The five components of the Stage 1: *Asking* Lesson Planner can be summarized as follows.

- 1A *Asking* Essential Skills: This is the central part of the tool, where the teacher uses the Skills Framework to identify which of the Essential or core *Asking* skills are going to be introduced or reinforced.

- 1B *Asking* Prerequisite Skills: Here the teacher considers which basic or foundational *Asking* skills need to be in place to complete the project. If there are skills that are not found in the Framework, the teacher can add them to the Essential Skills component under the section entitled "Skills to be introduced."

- 1C *Asking* Techniques Skills: Here the teacher considers which Skill Sets are being addressed and the best possible methods for developing questions.

- 1D *Asking* Equipment Needs (called "Technology Skills" in the Skills Framework): Here the teacher considers what equipment will be necessary to implement the *Asking* stage and makes a note to check that the equipment (e.g., overhead projector or computer hardware and software) is available and functioning properly.

- 1E *Asking* Review Skills: Here the teacher considers different ways to assess how the *Asking* stage was implemented and if the teacher's and student's goals for this stage were achieved; students are encouraged to self-assess their work here.

How Ms. Jones Uses the *Asking* Lesson Planner

Ms. Jones checks the Ten-Minute Lesson Planner for the Skill Sets that she had identified in the initial planning and then scans the complete Skills Framework to identify specific Essential *Asking* Skills that she wants to introduce to her students during the project. She circles Skill Set 3 for Thinking and Questioning under "1A *Asking* Essential Skills." Under this Skill Set she identifies skill (b) "uses personal interpretations of experiences, stories, poems, plays, or movies to generate questions" as the skill she would like to introduce. Having filled this in the central box entitled "1A *Asking* Essential Skills" under "Skills to be introduced" she moves to "1C *Asking* Techniques Skills" to consider ways to engage students in the topic. She circles "1. Brainstorming" and "2. Question Forming" as the two Skill Sets that she wishes to address. She brainstorms possible techniques or methods for fulfilling the goal of this component, which is to get students interested in the topic and have them ask their own questions; she fills in her ideas in the section entitled "Possible methods." She makes a note to give students the Student Basic *Asking* Tool. Now Ms. Jones considers the Technology Skills she will want to reinforce and fills in the section "1D *Asking* Equipment Needs."

Next, she moves to "1B *Asking* Prerequisite Skills" section and thinks through what skills she expects her student to have before they start the project. She also identifies two skills that she would like to reinforce at this stage and adds them to the *Asking* Essential Skills, under "Skills to be reinforced." Finally, she completes the fifth component of the *Asking* Lesson Planner, 1E *Asking* Review Skills. She identifies one skill that she would like to implement under the collaborative section of this component.

It is interesting to note that Ms. Jones moves through the various aspects of the Lesson Planner based on her own thinking rather than in a linear fashion. She goes back and forth between the various components until all five seem to fit together into a single cohesive strategy. Like the Ten-Minute Lesson Planner, this tool can be worked in any direction based on how the teacher thinks and plans.

The Student *Asking* Tools

Now let's turn our attention to the Student *Asking* Tools that Ms. Jones will use to encourage her students to become engaged in their learning and to improve their questioning skills.

Questions help to more clearly define the goals of any information task. The Student *Asking* tools presented in Figures 5.2 and 5.3 are designed to guide students to generate a list of key questions, which helps them to understand the parameters of the task. This in turn can lead to increased student involvement in new learning. It is important that the original teacher-initiated questions be embellished with specific questions developed through students' personal knowledge base, experiences, and natural interests. The sooner students key into the task at hand and become immersed in the assignment, the sooner they can take ownership of the entire process and are more likely to be willing to demonstrate the skills and knowledge they are acquiring.

Using Internet resources in project work is profoundly different from using books because of the ability to address specific questions of real interest on the Internet. For example, in a traditional paper-based project on beluga whales, students would probably be told to gather general information about beluga whales and create a report. This may result in students merely copying pages directly out of encyclopedias with minimal learning experience. Using the Internet in a Net-Savvy manner can provide real beginnings for students to ask intriguing questions of real personal interest. The nature of surfing helps students understand that there are multiple sources of information and points of view and thus many pathways to create personal connections in their learning.

As a teacher introduces a project on whales and describes the behavior of beluga whales, a student may ask, "Just how intelligent are beluga whales?" This simple question can become the basis of a unique effort on the part of this student. Although the assignment requires general information on beluga whales, it may do so only as a lead up to a report that provides evidence of how intelligent beluga whales really are. Doing an Internet search for material containing both "beluga" and "intelligence" yields an amazing amount of information that would not be found using traditional paper-based research methods.

Questions, especially those generated by learners, can become the starting point for unlocking knowledge whether it is contained in research projects or conversations with knowledgeable people. They lead to new ways of looking at things and can result in revelations, insights, or other forms of creative thinking. In the classroom, questioning that signals the awakening of a student's mind marks curiosity. This is the starting point for true learning. Having students generate questions is important, but equally important is helping them improve the quality of their questions. The Student *Asking* Tools can help on both accounts. This is done by having students move from asking questions that involve lower levels of thinking to higher levels of thinking. We do this by understanding that there are three types of content—content based on established knowledge, content based on current thinking, and content based on futuristic, speculative considerations.

Content based on established knowledge tends to deal with factual information from a perspective that has been accepted over a period of time and is generally considered as "conventional thinking." It may or may not be out of date with current thinking. Current trends, fashions, patterns, or fads give us insight into new ways of thinking. Current thinking, new ideas, and new theoretical knowledge provide us with the second type of content and becomes the basis of the third type of content. The third type of knowledge is one that is not yet established. It is future-focused and based on speculation, calculation, extrapolation, imagination, and so on. The Student Basic *Asking* Tool (Figure 5.2) deals mainly with asking questions that use factual, established content while the Student Higher-Level *Asking* Tool (Figure 5.3) helps students to ask questions that require current and futuristic, speculative type of content. Both tools are presented as worked examples done by Ms. Jones's student, Jessica Pembroke, who has teamed up with a group of students interested in doing the project on beluga whales. Blank versions of these tools are in Appendix B.

The purpose of the Student Basic *Asking* Tool is to ask questions that involve using mainly established knowledge, which can often, but not always, involve lower levels of thinking. The first part of the Basic *Asking* Tool, as shown in Figure 5.2, guides the student in the generation of a list of key words to be used in the creation of clarifying questions and questions of real interest to the student. For example, questioning words such as tell, recite, classify, recount, describe, and so on call upon established, historical knowledge. These key words also serve as the basis for the Stage 2: *Accessing* process, used to obtain data from the Internet, since these words become the basis of the "search language" students will use in the Internet search engines.

The three basic components of the Student Basic *Asking* Tool are summarized as follows.

- Topic: This is where the teacher aids in generating key words to help students think through basic questions.

- Background Questions: These are designed to help students recall their own past experiences and knowledge related to the topic or assignment.

- Clarifying Questions: These are the simple questions that involve recall, summarizing, and recounting of established knowledge.

Figure 5.2. Student Basic ASKING Tool

Project: *Whales*   **Teacher:** *Ms. Jones*   **Student(s):** *Jessica Pembroke*

Topic:
Teacher's key words on this topic:

whales
whale facts
dolphin whales
orcas whale
enemies

babies and family life
eating
killer whales
whale hunting
migration

---

1. Background Questions—based on your own knowledge (1A3b)

What general knowledge do you have about this topic? From where?
I saw Free Willy 3 times.
I like beluga whales the best.
My teacher made me do a report on grey whales in Grade 4.
I think it's wrong to eat whales or kill them for food.

Do you have any real world experiences or connections to this topic?
My mom has a carved whale tooth in her jewelry box.
My grandpa said in the old days he used to use whale oil to oil his watch.
I saw a white beluga whale at the aquarium and I saw them feed it.
My mom and dad ate beluga caviar once. I didn't like it at all so I spat it out.

What are your key words about this topic?
They have to be different from the teacher's, right?
beluga whales are very intelligent
baby belugas - I want to find out more about beluga whales, they are interesting

whale oil
feeding
aquarium
hunting
caviar

---

2. Clarifying Questions—based on established knowledge (1A3c)

Use the key words on this page to form questions that will guide you in finding established information about the topic. Try starting your questions with words like How do...?, What do...?, When...?, Why...?, Where do...? and Who...?

Q1. *What do beluga whales eat?*

Q2. *How much do they weigh? How big are they?*

Q3. *What do beluga whales look like?*

Q4. *How intelligent are belugas?*

Q5. *Do beluga whales migrate? Where?*

Q6. *Who are their enemies?*

Q7. *Where do they live?*

Q8. *Why do people call them belugas?*

Q9. *How do you get whale oil?*

Q10. *Why do people kill whales?*

Figure 5.3. Student Higher-Level ASKING Tool

Project: *Belugas*   **Teacher:** *Ms. Jones*   **Student(s):** *Jessica Pembroke*

3. Current Questions—based on present-day thinking (1A3d)
Much of the information available today is based on established knowledge that has been accepted for a period of time. It may or may not be out of date with current thinking. Prepare questions on your topic in light of current trends by contrasting the past with the present and questioning or wondering about how the topic could be looked at differently.

Q1. Why do we still hunt for and kill belugas today?

Q2. Are belugas different in size and weight than they were a hundred years ago? If so, why?

Q3. What is the difference between whale oil and synthetic oil? Can they do the same jobs?

Q4. Is it right or okay to keep large creatures such as whales in an aquarium?

Q5. Is it okay to eat beluga caviar?

4. Futuristic Questions—based on imaginative thinking (1A3e)
Consider the established and current knowledge on your topic, together with your personal knowledge, and try to predict things about your topic that may be true in the future. Prepare the questions by imagining, forecasting, pretending, amplifying, inventing, estimating, contrasting, explaining, extrapolating, or applying a principle, for example— How will...?, What if...?, If this... then what...?

Q1. What will happen to whales if we continue to hunt them?

Q2. What will happen to the migration habits of belugas if the Arctic water becomes warmer?

Q3. What if whales were really more intelligent than humans? How intelligent are they actually?

Q4.

Q5.

Note: In Figure 5.2 and subsequent worked samples of the tools, the numbers in brackets, e.g. "[1A3b]" and "[1A3e]" refer to the parts of the Skills Framework on which the material is based.

Some students may have difficulty answering one or more of these questions effectively. Others may find it difficult to show any initiative in drafting questions. For these students, the assignment may have to be reverted to a simpler basic form prescribed by the teacher, who can guide them and help them until they can start asking their own questions. Some students may pose current-day thinking or futuristic questions under the "Clarifying Questions" section of the tool. These questions can be transferred to the Student Higher-Level *Asking* Tool later if it is used. Jessica does use this tool as her curiosity leads her to ask these types of questions as shown in Figure 5.3.

The Student Higher-Level *Asking* Tool asks questions that require a student to think through current and future knowledge. Moving to questions about things happening right now involves analysis of current trends, patterns, and events. Questions based on current thinking require the use of higher levels of thinking and synthesis since the information is still in the processing stage and not yet established as knowledge. Questions requiring analysis of current thinking include descriptors such as reason, analyze, evaluate, judge, distinguish, match, compare, and so on.

However, it is questions based on the future that involve the highest levels of thinking. We have to dream, project, extrapolate, predict, and use our imaginations and predictive powers to the fullest. This is a hard thing to learn and harder to do well. Future-based questions include descriptors such as imagine, speculate, amplify, forecast, and hypothesize. When we generate questions, it is important that we use a mixture of all three types of questions, including those that call upon established knowledge, as well as those that require current and future-based information. This way we can access and use all levels of thinking—from the highest to the lowest.

Chapter 6

Stage 2: *ACCESSING—Teacher and Student Tools*

In this chapter we introduce two tools, the Stage 2: *Accessing* Lesson Planner (Figure 6.1) for teachers and the Student *Accessing* Tool for Search Engines (Figure 6.2). Both tools are presented as worked examples. Blank versions of the tools that can be photocopied for use are in the Appendixes.

Stage 2: *Accessing* Lesson Planner

The Stage 2: *Accessing* Lesson Planner, shown in Figure 6.1, is used with the Ten-Minute Lesson Planner, which is described in Chapter 4 as well as the Stage 1: *Asking* Lesson Planner. The purpose of the *Accessing* Lesson Planner is to help teachers plan the integration of specific *Accessing* skills into the objectives of any instructional unit or project. The *Accessing* Lesson Planner is a detailed extension of the *Accessing* component of the Ten-Minute Lesson Planner, where the teacher identified general *Accessing* Skill Sets to be addressed during the project. Using the *Accessing* Lesson Planner, the teacher identifies the specific *Accessing* skills to be introduced and/or reinforced. These skills are organized under the *Accessing* Skill Sets of the complete Skills Framework, which is located in Part III.

Figure 6.1 shows a completed version of Ms. Jones's lesson plan for implementing the *Accessing* stage. The Stage 2: *Accessing* Lesson Planner is structured in exactly the same way as the *Asking* Lesson Planner, which was described in the previous chapter. The *Accessing* Lesson Planner has the same five components, which are designed to work with the five major components of the *Accessing* Skills Framework. Structurally, each of the components in the Planner outlines the goal of the component, gives a summary of the skill sets in that component, and lists the sections related to planning the implementation of that component. Figure 6.1 shows how Ms. Jones has used this tool. The five components of the Stage 2: *Accessing* Lesson Planner are as follows.

- 2A *Accessing* Essential Skills: This is the central part of the tool, where the teacher uses the Skills Framework to identify which of the Essential or core *Accessing* skills are going to be introduced or reinforced.

- 2B *Accessing* Prerequisite Skills: Here the teacher considers which basic *or* foundational *Accessing* skills need to be in place to complete the project. If there are skills that are not found in the Framework, the teacher can add them to the Essential Skills component under the section entitled "Skills to be introduced."

- 2C *Accessing* Techniques Skills: Here the teacher considers possible methods for students to research the topic for the project.

Figure 6.1. Stage 2: ACCESSING Lesson Planner

2B. Accessing Prerequisite Skills

Goal: to check your assumptions about what basic Accessing skills students must already have

Basic Student Skills Needed

1. General Workstation
2. General Computer
3. General Internet
4. Internet On-line
5. General Reading
6. Technical Reading

Check that students have:

2B1- General Workstation Skill Set

2B2- General Computer Skill Set - check both

Review:

2B4- On-line Internet Skill Set - Netiquette Skills

Add any basic skills that are not included in the Skills Framework to the Essential Skills section below

2C. Accessing Techniques Skills

Goal: to examine possible methods of Accessing data and choosing the best for this project

Possible Methods

Student Accessing Tool for Search Engines
Student Analyzing Tool for Web sites
Student Analyzing Tool for Documenting Sources

Accessing the Internet:

1. Starting Skills
2. Indexing Systems
3. Sources by Location
4. Communication
5. Sources—Real time
6. Primary Sources
7. Secondary Sources
8. Traditional Sources

- *recalling previous knowledge*
- *Internet searches*
- *Internet primary sources if possible*
- *paper-based sources*

2A. Accessing Essential Skills

Goal: to identify the skills you want students to develop during the Accessing stage of the project

1. Using Hardware
2. Using Software
3. Recording Data and Creating a Bibliography

Skills to be introduced

- *2A2(b) Internet browser skills for navigating the Internet, entering and using URLs, and using hypertext links to locate and download data*
- *2A2(f) Internet search engine tips (focus on sifting to get primary sites, such as aquariums or institutions with access to living killer or beluga whales)*

Skills to be reinforced

- *2B4 Using proper Netiquette*

2D. Accessing Equipment Needs

Goal: to make sure that the equipment needed for Accessing sources is available and working properly

1. Software Needs

a. Word processor   b. Database   c. Spreadsheet
d. Scanners   e. Photos   f. OCR   g. Voice recognition

check search engine software

2. Hardware needs

a. ISP   b. Computer   c. WebTV   d. Backup storage
e. CDROM   f. Multimedia   g. LAN   h. Modem   i. Scanner
j. VCR   k. Camera   l. Tape recorder   m. Video camera

book time in computer room

2E. Accessing Reviewing Skills

Goal: to check that the Accessing processes are properly and fully implemented

1. Student Process Review

2. Collaborative Process Review

3. Teacher Process Review

ask students to hand in their accessing tools to determine how effectively they have accessed Internet sites

- 2D *Accessing* Equipment Needs (called "Technology Skills" in the Skills Framework): Here the teacher considers what equipment will be necessary to implement the *Accessing* stage and makes a note to check that the equipment (e.g., computer hardware and software) is available and functioning properly.

- 2E *Accessing* Review Skills: Here the teacher considers how to assess how well the *Accessing* stage was implemented and if the teacher's and students' goals for this stage were achieved. Students are encouraged to self-assess their own work here.

How Ms. Jones Uses the *Accessing* Lesson Planner

Ms. Jones checks the Ten-Minute Lesson Planner for the Skill Sets that she had identified in the initial planning and then scans the complete Skills Framework to identify specific Essential *Accessing* Skills that she wants to introduce to her students during the project. As she did in Stage 1: *Asking*, she moves through the various aspects of the Lesson Planner based on her own thinking rather than in a linear fashion. She goes back and forth between the various components until all five seem to fit together into a single cohesive strategy.

She circles Skill Set 3 for "Recording Data and Creating a Bibliography" under "2A *Accessing* Essential Skills" as shown in Figure 6.1. Under this Skill Set she identifies skill "2A 2 (b) Internet browser skills for navigating the Internet, entering and using URLs, and using hypertext links to locate and download data" as the skill she would like to introduce. Next, in box "2B *Accessing* Prerequisite Skills" she circles Skill Sets 1 to 4 as the prerequisite sets and identifies Skill Set 4 (Netiquette) as the one that needs to be reinforced and adds it to "2A *Accessing* Essential Skills," under "Skills to be reinforced." Then Ms. Jones moves to "2C *Accessing* Techniques Skills" to consider the best possible ways of accessing data on whales. Under the section "Possible Methods" she decides to use all of the student tools, and for accessing the Internet, circles "6. Primary Sources" and "8. Traditional Sources." Next, she considers what equipment will be needed to complete the project under "2D *Assessing* Equipment Needs" by referring to the "2D *Accessing* Technology" section in the complete Skills Framework. Finally, she completes the fifth component of this Planner, "2E *Accessing* Review Skills." She plans how she will review the process that has been followed to complete the *Accessing* stage of the NetSavvy process.

The Student *Accessing* Tools

Once the information needs of the assignment are established in the *Asking* Stage, in the *Accessing* Stage the student sets about to acquire data to answer these questions. Although the focus of this book is on using the Internet for this purpose, most assignments can and do involve the accessing of other sources of information, and all of the NetSavvy tools can be adapted for that purpose. In the paper-based world, a student doing an assignment on whales may have consulted a few books and a standard encyclopedia or two. Today, with so much information available on the Internet, there is an important new issue to address. Before we present the Student *Accessing* Tool (Figure 6.2) we need to spend time addressing some important aspects of using the Internet for on-line searching. For example, how is a student to sort through the thousands of available Web sites to find the very best ones?

This key question is answered using a variety of techniques, some of which have already been introduced. First, in the *Asking* stage, it was important to be clear about exactly what the student was to look for. Second, in the *Accessing* stage, the appropriate "search language" must be used in the right ways. Developing appropriate search language and learning to use "search engines" effectively is central to accessing good and relevant data and reducing InfoWhelm. In the *Accessing* stage, the skillful use of Internet search engines and directories comes into play. Let's first turn our attention to some important issues around Internet search engines that help us to find on-line information. This involves learning how to choose the best search engine for your purpose and understanding the functions of directories, metacrawlers, and question-answering search engines.

Internet Search Engines

The focus of the Stage 2: Student *Accessing* Tool is the use of Internet search engines. Let's take a moment to consider some of the dozens of search engines on the Internet. Search engines are basically indexes of Web pages (*Web* is used interchangeably with *Internet*, but, the Web is the graphical part of the text-based Internet) compiled by computers that spend all their time trying to access every word in every Web site on the Internet. The different search engines take different approaches and are evolving with time as they compete with each other for different niches. For the most up-to-date information on the current state of the race and for dozens of pages explaining the many differences between search engines and how best to use them, just type URL: searchenginewatch into your browser's location bar and hit the return key.

Although many people understand search engines to be basically the same, there are significant differences. Consider some of the largest search engines:

- AltaVista
- Northern Light
- Inktomi (used by Hotbot, and others)
- Fast
- Excite
- Lycos
- Go-InfoSeek
- WebCrawler

Consider three engines, AltaVista, Excite, and WebCrawler, and the number of Web pages that they had indexed as of March 2000. If you type in the word "whale," you get significant differences in the number of hits or "Web results." Table 6.1 summarizes these results.

Table 6.1. Comparison Between AltaVista, Excite, and WebCrawler Search Engines, in Terms of Pages Indexed and Results of a Search on the Word *"Whale"*

Search Engine	Number of Pages Indexed	Number of Results
AltaVista	250 million	526,580 listings of Web pages
Excite	120 million	140,000 hits
WebCrawler	4 million	5,538 Web results

These differences can be significant. You may want to try typing the same search words into different engines* and comparing the results, or going to URL: searchenginewatch or Nueva Library Help to read comparative data and descriptions.

Nueva Library Help offers a summary chart showing the strengths of different search engines, and a version of this is shown in Table 6.2. For details explaining more about the characteristics of each engine mentioned and a current version of this chart, go to the Web site at:

URL: http://www.nueva.pvt.k12.ca.us/~debbie/library/research/
adviceengine.html#broad

By visiting this site and clicking on the engine names listed, you can go directly to them. Don't be overwhelmed by this chart. It has been included merely to indicate some of the range of search engines available today. In our example, Ms. Jones will only use the largest search engine, AltaVista, for her "whales" project. For our purposes AltaVista is a good general all-around starting point to learn how to use a search engine.

Internet Directories

Wondering why Yahoo hasn't been mentioned yet? Although Yahoo is a more popular search method, it is not a computer-generated search engine. Yahoo, Snap, Netscape's Open Directory, and Lycos are old-fashioned human-created directories or lists of categories displayed in electronic form. Yahoo's search feature responds first as a directory, but its Web site actually calls itself an Internet Guide, since it is a hybrid of a directory and a search engine. Yahoo explains the difference between the two in terms of a book analogy: a directory is like a table of contents, while a search engine is like an index.

If you type the word "whale" into AltaVista's search engine you get a listing of over 522,000+ Web pages, but if you type "whale" into Yahoo you first get a listing of 40 categories, such as:

/Science/Biology/Zoology/Animals_Insects_and_Pets/Marine_Life
/Marine_Mammals/Whale

---

*Tip: The easiest way to access most search engines is to just type its name into your Web browser's location bar. It is not usually necessary to type in the official URL (URL is an Internet address and an acronym for Uniform Resource Locator), for example, AltaVista's URL: http://www.altavista.com. Merely typing in "altavista" and touching the return key will get you to the AltaVista home page immediately.

Table 6.2. Choosing the Best Internet Search Device for Your Purpose

Your Purpose	*Internet Search Device*
To narrow a broad topic	Yahoo Northern Lights
Fast access to relevant hits and a good idea of what's on each page	Google Excite
Overview multiple engines for an idea of what's available for a topic	Dogpile
Quality, evaluated sites	Magellan Lycos TOP 5% Home WebCrawler
Narrow term to pinpoint search	AltaVista
Encyclopedia-type information	Information Please Entertainment Almanac Sports Almanac Columbia Encyclopedia Random House College Dictionary
Keywords which appear in many documents	HotBot
Common words in a phrase need to be included in my search	Infoseek
Information on an event (I know the date)	HotBot Super Search
Web pages in or about a programming language	HotBot Super Search
Accurate information for a school project that I can take home or on the bus	Nueva's library catalogue ProQuest Direct
Scientific information (e.g., to back up the research for my science fair project)	AltaVista
Mathematics or statistics information	MathSearch
To search in natural language; I can describe my topic in a sentence	InfoSeek Ask Jeeves
Information on a proper name (a place, person, or object)	AltaVista InfoSeek HotBot
Web pages from a geographic region	MetaCrawler
Web pages from an Internet domain (e.g., schools)...	HotBot Super Search
Images or sounds	Columbia University's WebSEEK AltaVista Photo Finder Lycos Media HotBot: SuperSearch The Amazing Picture Machine Yahoo! Computers and Internet:Multimedia:Pictures, Arriba Vista
Quotations	The Quotations Page, Bartlett, Land of Quotes
Advice and opinions	Reference.Com, Deja News also Usenet posts & discussion groups
I bet this search has been done before...	Ask Jeeves!
To browse	A2Z, Yahoo
Just for kids	Yahooligans!

SOURCE: Nueva Library Help at URL:
http://www.nueva.pvt.k12.ca.us/~debbie/library/research/adviceengine.html#broad

Following this link will take you to a page of descriptive titles such as "Whale songs—educational center about people and whales." Clicking on this title will take you to the Whale Songs Web site. It should be noted that although AltaVista presents itself as a search engine, immediately following its first 10 hits it also presents a simple directory function. Jessica discovers that the title "AltaVista Recommends;" offers up categories such as "Ecotourism>Whale Watching."

The Web site URL: searchengine.com observes that "because of the human role, directories can often provide better results than search engines." Many people find that having Web sites organized into categories is a very helpful way to get an overview of the search results. Yahoo is the largest directory on the Internet and in 1999 was the most popular search service on the Web.

Metacrawlers

What about Dogpile, Go2Net, MetaCrawler, or, if you have a Macintosh computer, Sherlock? These are examples of super search engines known as metacrawlers. Despite having no database of their own, they will search on your behalf through the indexes of any number of search engines and compile the results into one super list. This is a great feature that saves you from having to input your search data into a number of different search engines, one after the other.

Question-Answering Engines

What about Ask Jeeves! and other search engines where you can type whole questions and receive a list of Web sites likely to answer the question? Ask Jeeves! usually responds like a MetaCrawler and uses a variety of search engines to come up with Web sites likely to contain the answer to your question. There are sites specifically for answering children's questions, such as Ask Jeeves for Kids!, Disney Internet Guide, and Yahooligans, that will not return Web sites considered inappropriate for children.

If you type into Ask Jeeves! "What is the state capital of California?" it responds with a button labeled "Where can I find government information of the type 'the capital and state facts' for the state 'California'." When you click on this it takes you to a site with the correct answer. However, typing in AltaVista "+ 'state capital' + 'California" gets almost identical results since AltaVista responds with a button labeled "AltaVista knows the answers to these questions: What are the 50 states and their capitals?" Once again, this example illustrates how search devices differ in a variety of ways and how they have complex capabilities subject to frequent revision. It is not possible to generalize very much about what each can or cannot do so the advice is to check them out and decide which ones suit your purpose!

Basic Rules for Searches Engines

The home page of any search engine is set up to do what is called a **simple search**. Usually there is a nearby option offering the user the choice to do an **advanced**

search. Some teachers or students may feel they do not want to stay in the minor leagues using a mere simple search engine and want to move to an advanced search as soon as possible. The names are a little misleading since the simple search category embodies sophisticated search techniques. As AltaVista points out on its Advanced Search Help page:

> Advanced search is for very specific searches and not for general searching. Almost everything you need to search for can be found quickly and with better results by using the standard search box where AltaVista search services sorts the results by placing the most relevant content first.

This means that getting 2 million hits is not necessarily a bad thing, since the first 10 hits shown on your screen will probably contain many of the most relevant sites for you out of a list of 2 million. This is good news because it allows you to discard the rest if you choose. For our purposes the simple search will be more than adequate, and we can leave the so-called advanced search for people who have extra time to delve into the details of its refinements!

Let us now turn to considering the conventions and basic rules that search engines use to retrieve data. These conventions include the use of plus and minus signs, lowercase, and wild cards. Read on!

Using Plus Signs and Minus Signs

If Jessica types any two words into a search engine, it will return sites containing *either* or *both* of the words. Usually she would want only sites containing both words, so using a plus sign (+) ensures that the word following it *must* appear in a Web site for it to be listed in her results. Similarly, a minus sign (−) in front of a word will eliminate any site containing that word from the resulting list.

Using Lowercase Normally

If Jessica types search words into a search engine without using capital letters, she will get back hits containing all case forms of a word, whether they contain capitals or not. However, if she uses capitals in some search engines, lowercase listings of the word may not be returned. As a result the general rule is always to use lowercase words in search engines. For example, consider these results from AltaVista:

whale	yields 516,020 Web pages (this yields all cases)
Whale	yields 287,790 Web pages (exact matches only)
WHALE	yields 40,110 Web pages (exact matches only)
wHALE	yields 5 Web pages (exact matches only)

Using the Wildcard Symbol, the Asterisk (*)

This feature also serves to remind the user of how literal search engines can be about interpreting what is typed in. When Jessica tried "+whale +beluga" she got about 18,000 hits, but when she typed in "+whale +belugas" she got only about

3,000 hits, probably since "beluga whales" (no 's' on beluga) is more commonly categorized than just "belugas." The way around this is to remember to use the asterisk (*) symbol frequently.

Using "beluga*" will return any form of the word beluga, such as "belugas," "belugawhale," "belugafood," or "belugawhatever." In the case above using the totally open form "+whale* +beluga*" will yield a more fruitful 25,000 Web sites. For some purposes this last method of entry might be more useful than trying natural phrases such as "beluga whales" which yields about 2,400 Web sites, or "beluga whale" which yields about 1,700 Web sites. Again, try it out and you will see what we mean!

Introducing the Student *Accessing* Tool for Search Engines

The purpose of the Student *Accessing* Tool is to help students maximize the use of search engines to locate good data. The *Accessing* tool guides a student in doing three types of searches:

- General search
- Specific search
- Exact phrase search

Internet searching involves two contrary-sounding goals: maximizing the number of hits on your subject while minimizing the number of hits not on your subject. Ideally you want to maximize the number of hits on your subject and minimize the number of hits not on your subject, at the same time.

How can you quickly measure how well you are doing? By examining your first page of results for "good" (relevant) hits and "bad" (irrelevant) hits. Let us examine Jessica's experience in searching for information on her topic, beluga whales. Her trials and results are summarized in Figure 6.2.

In our worked example of the *Accessing* Tool, Jessica's goal is to get 100% good hits on her first page of results. In the first part of the *Accessing* Tool Jessica does a "General Search" using the obvious key word "beluga" in the AltaVista search engine and gets a result of over 30,000 hits. Three of the first five hits she reads confuse and distract her. They are "Beluga Computing," and "Beluga Consultancy" (both company names), and the home page of a German shepherd dog trainer by the name of "Presley von Beluga." She has just discovered the problem with doing a very general search—too many bad hits.

It should be noted that because Jessica merely typed in "beluga" she missed all the sites that are indexed with the word "belugas" (plural). To solve this problem and maximize the number of good hits, Jessica tries again by ending her search word with the asterisk (*), which will yield sites containing all forms of the words beginning "beluga. ..." Typing in beluga* returns about 50% more hits, over 45,000.

Next she tries typing in "whales beluga" and gets 38,820 hits—sites containing the word "beluga," *or* the word "whale," *or* both. Jessica thinks she's lucky because

Figure 6.2. Student ACCESSING Tool for Search Engines (2A2)

Accessing topic: *Whales/Belugas*   **Student(s):** *Jessica Pembroke*

Search engine name (to be entered in Web browser location bar): *altavista*

A. GENERAL SEARCH for ___*beluga whales*___

Make sure you use lower case and end your words with an asterisk (*) to avoid missing pluralized and other versions of your keywords.

Search language	Hits	Comments
1. *beluga*	hits: *30,780*	*poor - sites with only "beluga"*
2. *beluga**	hits: *45,310*	*better - all word forms of beluga(s).*
3. *+beluga* +whales**	hits: *19,180*	*best - sites with both words, in many forms, but with fewer irrelevant hits*
4.	hits:	

B. SPECIFIC SEARCH for ___*what do beluga whales eat?*___

Remember, for specific information, type in enough key words to narrow down the number of hits to the exact information you are looking for.

Search language	Hits	Comment
1. *beluga* whales* food**	hits: *400,950*	*inaccurate number of real hits*
2. *+beluga* +whale* +food**	hits: *11,781*	*study hits for better key words, too many irrelevant words about beluga caviar*
3. *+beluga* +whale* +diet**	hits: *4,081*	*better - lots of good hits*
4.	hits:	

C. EXACT PHRASE SEARCH for ___*beluga whales eat*___

Now do an exact search using "quotation marks" around the key phrase of your question.

Search language	Hits	Comment
1. *"beluga whales eat"*	hits: *0*	*revise words and try again*
2. *"belugas eat"*	hits: *12*	*good hits about what belugas eat*
3.	hits:	
4.	hits:	

the first five hits all look like good ones that deal directly with beluga whales. This is not luck, since AltaVista presents the hits "in order" of what it perceives or thinks you are looking for. In this case AltaVista assumes the search is for "beluga" *and* "whales." Really, if Jessica wanted to do a specific search for just "beluga whales" she should have used the plus sign (+) feature to narrow the search down to a greater number of relevant hits.

Out of curiosity she reverses the words and tries again using "beluga whales" and gets only 2,400 hits, as if she somehow managed to avoid sites with just one word or the other. The result is similar to using the exact phrase "'belugawhales.'" It seems to indicate that most beluga whale sites have been categorized under the two-word phrase "'beluga whales.'" Although you might have expected more focused results compared with the first search, both searches yielded the same first 10 hits in the same order since AltaVista always lists the best hits first (namely those containing both beluga and whales). This somewhat confusing exercise shows that word order is not important for getting good hits, but it is important if you want an accurate picture of the number of real hits pertaining to a two-word subject.

While Jessica was initially happy just to look at general sites about "beluga whales," she eventually finds she is still missing an answer to a specific question, "What do beluga whales eat?"

When Jessica does a search for beluga* whale* food* AltaVista returns 400,950 Web pages containing *any* or *all* of these words. If Jessica types in the same words using plus signs: +beluga* +whale* +food,* the plus sign ensures that the word following it *must* appear in a Web site for it to be listed in her results. Using plus signs yields a far more accurate picture of the number of Web pages containing information on the topic "beluga food"; about 12,000 hits, or just 3% of the 400,950 Web sites obtained in the first search. The first Web site and many of the others listed in the 12,000 mentioned above were about the food product beluga caviar, which comes from sturgeon, and not from beluga whales. Since this expensive delicacy is plainly not a food that beluga whales eat, the search could be done again as "+beluga* +food* -caviar*." In this case you get an even more accurate result, about 5,000 relevant hits, the first of which is exactly what you want, a site about the "diet and eating habits" of beluga whales.

This example illustrates the care with which a search sometimes should be done, since both the words "food" and "beluga" had ambiguous meanings in the situation described above. We probably didn't realize we would end up with a lot of sites featuring "beluga" as a food and not sites about food that belugas eat or that we would get lots of sites about "beluga" that were not about beluga whales.

At this point Jessica realizes using "+beluga" "+whale*," and "+diet" would have been a better starting point. Sure enough, using these three words yields 4,081 hits containing both these words. Jessica may conclude that choosing key words carefully is a good strategy.

Another way to do a specific search is to do an "exact phrase search." Jessica tries this strategy for finding what food beluga whales like to eat. She suspects that some of the thousands of Internet sites on beluga whales will contain the phrase "beluga whales eat. . ." and tries this out by placing these words in quotation marks in the search engine. This effort yields zero hits, but she doesn't give up. She tries again using "belugas eat" and is delighted to get just 12 hits, some of which are perfect.

If you are really confused, relax. Search engines have their own idiosyncrasies but once you learn some of their operational words and signs, they work well. It's just a matter of learning one or two well, rather than trying to work with too many. We have just given you one example; if you are sick of hearing the word "beluga" try looking up something more interesting, like chocolate!

Closing Comments

In the pre-Internet world it was very difficult to get material published, especially material that was to be used in schools. The process was long and difficult. As a result, it denied most students access to the work of most writers. Today, students can access millions of sources on the Internet, and students are even free to publish any material on the Internet themselves. This amazing broadening of the opportunity to publish does have a downside. The old filtering mechanisms that served to eliminate suspect materials do not exist at all on the Internet, and the business of filtering has become the responsibility of the user.

If a student finds a Web site that seems to contain good answers to the questions being researched, it is best to record the useful information and to document the source. We provide a tool to do just this, and it is given the name of Student *Analyzing* Tool for Documenting Sources. Since this is an analysis function, the tool is presented in the next chapter (Chapter 7) under the section on Student *Analyzing* Tools.

There are two possibilities for using the Student *Analyzing* Tool for Documenting Sources when a student is using the Internet—during the process of accessing Internet site or later off-line. To use this *Analyzing* tool off-line a student would have to print out pages documenting sources and authors at the time a site is visited. Alternatively, it would be necessary to fill in the Student *Analyzing* tool together with the Student *Accessing* Tool while a Web site is being accessed. It should be noted that this involves doing parts of Stage 2 *Accessing* and Stage 3 *Analyzing* together.

Chapter 7

Stage 3: ANALYZING—Teacher and Student Tools

In this chapter we introduce three tools—the Stage 3: *Analyzing* Lesson Planner (Figure 7.1) for teachers, the Student *Analyzing* Tool for Web Sites (Figure 7.2), and the Student *Analyzing* Tool for Documenting Sources (Figure 7.3). All three tools are presented as worked examples. Blank versions that can be photocopied for use are found in the Appendixes.

Stage 3: *Analyzing* Lesson Planner

The Stage 3: *Analyzing* Lesson Planner, shown in Figure 7.1, is used with the Ten-Minute Lesson Planner, which is described in Chapter 4, as well as the Stage 1: *Asking* Lesson Planner and the Stage 2: *Accessing* Lesson Planner. The purpose of the *Analyzing* Lesson Planner is to help the teacher plan the integration of specific *Analyzing* stage skills into the objectives of any instructional unit or project. The *Analyzing* Lesson Planner is a detailed extension of the *Analyzing* component of the Ten-Minute Lesson Planner, where the teacher identified general *Analyzing* Skill Sets to be addressed during the project. Using the *Analyzing* Lesson Planner, the teacher identifies the specific *Analyzing* skills to be introduced and/or reinforced. These skills are organized under the *Analyzing* Skill Sets of the complete Skills Framework, which is located in Part III.

Figure 7.1 shows a completed version of Ms. Jones' lesson plan for implementing the *Analyzing* stage. The Stage 3: *Analyzing* Lesson Planner is structured in exactly the same way as the *Asking* and *Accessing* Lesson Planners, which were described in the previous two chapters. The *Analyzing* Lesson Planner has the same five components, which are designed to work with the five major components of the *Analyzing* Skills Framework. Structurally, each of the components in the Planner outlines the goal of the component, gives a summary of the skill sets in that component, and lists the sections related to planning the implementation of that component. Figure 7.1 shows how Ms. Jones has used this tool. The five components of the Stage 3: *Analyzing* Lesson Planner can be summarized as follows.

- 3A *Analyzing* Essential Skills: This is the central part of the tool, where the teacher uses the Skills Framework to identify which of the Essential or core *Analyzing* skills are going to be introduced or reinforced.

- 3B *Analyzing* Prerequisite Skills: Here the teacher considers which basic or foundational skills need to be in place to complete the project. If there are skills that are not found in the Framework, the teacher can add them

Figure 7.1. Stage 3: ANALYZING Lesson Planner

3B. Analyzing **Prerequisite Skills**

Goal: to check your assumptions about what basic Analyzing skills students should already have

Basic Student Skills Needed

1. General Thinking skills
   - *3B1 General Thinking Skill Set*

2. Critical Thinking skills
   - *3B2 Critical Thinking Skill Set*

Add any basic skills that are not included in the Skills Framework to the Essential Skills section below

3C. Analyzing **Techniques Skills**

Goal: to consider the best possible methods of Analyzing data

Possible Methods

Student Analyzing Tool for Web sites
Student Analyzing Tool for Documenting

a. Diagramming	b. Webs	c. Categorizing
d. Outlining	e. Paraphrasing	f. Sequencing
g. Note cards	h. Databases	i. Spreadsheets

- *summarize Internet searches on note cards*
- *use cards to create whole database*
- *create outline for report*

3A. Analyzing **Essential Skills**

Goal: to identify the analyzing, documenting and authenticating skills you want students to develop during the Analyzing stage of the project

1. General Analyzing	2. Critical Analyzing	3. Media Analyzing
4. General Authenticating	5. Internet Documenting	6. Critical Authenticating

Skills to be introduced

- *3A1(e) Considers different perspectives provided by data sources*
- *3A1(f) Considers sources that provide alternative points of view*

Skills to be reinforced

- *3B1(d) Sifts to recover good data and reject bad data*
- *3B2(d) Questions the relevance of the data*

3D. Analyzing **Equipment Needs**

Goal: to make sure that the equipment needed for Analyzing information is available and working

1. Software needs
a. Diagramming software

b. Idea & concept mapping software
- *word processor optional*

2. Hardware Needs
- *computers optional*

3. Other
- *student uses printouts from Accessing stage and transfers to notecards to create database*

3E. Analyzing **Reviewing Skills**

Goal: to check that the Analyzing processes are properly and fully implemented

1. Student Process Review

2. Collaborative Process Review

3. Teacher Process Review
- *review quality of student note cards*

to the Essential Skills component under the section entitled "Skills to be introduced."

- 3C *Analyzing* Techniques Skills: Here the teacher considers which Skills Sets are being addressed and the best possible methods for analyzing the data that will be accessed.

- 3D *Analyzing* Equipment Needs (called "Technology Skills" in the Skills Framework): Here possible hardware and software that can be used for the purpose of analysis are considered. This is done so that hardware and software usage aligns with the other components of the *Analyzing* Lesson Planner, particularly the Techniques and Essential Skills components.

- 3E *Analyzing* Review Skills: Here the teacher considers how the student, team members, or others, as well as the teacher, can assess how well the other four stages of *Analyzing* were implemented and learned.

How Ms. Jones Uses the *Analyzing* Lesson Planner

Ms. Jones checks the Ten-Minute Lesson Planner for the Skill Sets that she had identified in the initial planning and then examines the complete Skills Framework to identify specific Essential *Analyzing* Skills that she wants to introduce to her students during the "whales" project. She moves through the various aspects of the Lesson Planner based on her own thinking rather than in a linear fashion. She goes back and forth between the various components until all five seem to fit together into a single cohesive strategy.

The Student *Analyzing* Tools

Next let's consider two Student *Analyzing* Tools—the Student *Analyzing* Tool for Web Sites and the Student *Analyzing* Tool for Documenting Sources. These tools are specifically designed to help students analyze information that they find at Web sites, as well as to track, document, and authenticate information sources.

The Student *Analyzing* Tool for Web Sites

The Student *Analyzing* Tool for Web Sites shown in Figure 7.2 is a checklist that prompts a student to consider a number of ways to establish the credibility of a Web site. As we all know, there are good Web sites, mediocre Web sites, and bad Web sites. For a student looking for data about beluga whales, a good Web site is one that provides general data and supplies answers to the student's specific questions. While doing this, the student should be attempting to confirm that the Web site itself has a degree of credibility, that the author's identity can be established, and that there is a method of confirming or challenging the data provided.

The purpose of Student *Analyzing* Tool for Web Sites is to help students qualitatively and quantitatively analyze the merits and/or demerits of a Web site. Figure 7.2

Figure 7.2. Student ANALYZING Tool for Web Sites

Student(s): *Jessica Pembroke* **Website:** *New York Aquarium* **http**://*wcsorg/zoos/aquarium*

	pick one	Explain your choice
Content (3A5e)		
1. Content excellent for your purpose	[5]	
2. Content good for your purpose	[4]	
3. Content helpful for your purpose	(3)	*not much organized infomation, but got a*
4. Content poor for your purpose	[2]	*few good facts I can use*
5. Content irrelevant for your purpose	[1]	
Organization Links		
1. Web page of an organization/institute	(5)	*New York Aquarium*
2. Web site linked to organization/institute	[4]	
3. A large independent Web site	[3]	
4. Small Web site with some simple links	[2]	
5. No relation to anything else	[1]	
Authorship (3A5c)		
1. Author has reputation and credentials	[5]	
2. Author has interest and credentials	[4]	
3. Author has special interest in subject	[3]	
4. Author not very knowledgeable	[2]	
5. Author unknown	(1)	*hard to tell, voluteers answer questions*
Sources (3A4f)		
1. Material is writer's own research	[5]	
2. Material is based on primary sources	[4]	
3. Material closely linked to credible source	[3]	
4. Material seems based on secondary sources	(2)	*very few facts*
5. Sources unknown	[1]	
Authentication of information		
1. Author can be queried by e-mail	[5]	
2. Site can be reached by e-mail	(4)	*you can send questions to:*
3. Site or author can be reached by mail	[3]	*Friends of the Aquarium at fpzewcsorg*
4. Site or author can be reached by other means	[2]	
5. No way to reach author or the site	[1]	
Presentation (3A5f)		
1. Web site is appealing or impressive	[5]	
2. Web site is perfectly fine for its purpose	(4)	*nice beluga photo*
3. Focus is on presentation and not content	[3]	
4. Weak on content and presentation	[2]	
5. Very minimal effort on presentation	[1]	
Total Web site quality adds up to	*19*/30	

Please add up your choices from each section. Circle the corresponding number and rating.

6 7 8 9 10	11 12 13 14 15	16 17 18 (19) 20	21 22 23 24 25	26 27 28 29 30
AWFUL	POOR	(SATISFACTORY)	GOOD	EXCELLENT

shows a worked example of this tool. Once again, this is the work of Ms. Jones' student Jessica Pembroke. There are six components that make up this tool.

- Content: This provides choices on how to evaluate the relevance of the content to the task or assignment.
- Organization Link: This asks the student to consider what kind of organization this Web site is linked to or affiliated with.
- Authorship: This component asks the student to question the qualifications and authority of the creator or writer.
- Sources: Here the student is required to think about what kind of source this is.
- Authentication of Information: This component asks the student to determine the accessibility of the author to the researcher.
- Presentation: Here student is asked to evaluate a general impression of the site and the manner in which the information has been presented.

This tool is purposely broad in terms of categories, but specific in terms of prompts. It takes into account the purpose of the assignment and asks students to consider how well a specific site addresses their information needs. Each component of the Student *Analyzing* Tool for Web Sites can be given up to 5 marks based on how effective that aspect is. Space is also provided for comments so that students have to consider the reasons why they rate a Web site a certain way. Jessica Pembroke rates this Web site at 19 out of 30, which is classified as a "Satisfactory" site. Based on her commentary in the "Comments" sections, it is easy to see why she rated the site the way she did.

It should be noted that Web sites that are created by students should not be used as sources, since the material is usually third hand, and the credibility of a student author is usually not as high as that of other readily available sources. Sites linked to scientific institutions or organizations will immediately have considerable credibility, but the work of highly interested and experienced individuals should also be seriously investigated as well.

The Student *Analyzing* Tool for Documenting Sources

The freedom and relatively low cost of the Internet allow almost any person, anywhere, to publish anything, anytime. Whether the person is right or wrong, ignorant or wise, well intentioned or not, none of this is necessarily a factor in what gets published on the Internet. It should be noted that the more errors, deceptions, and misconceptions that invade primary sources, the more these bad data are then copied and repeated in secondary and tertiary sources. Bad data may be transmitted by inexperienced individuals with no harmful intent as well as by those fully intent on the distribution of misinformation. In either case, they have more credibility than the primary sources, thus lending increased authority to errors, deceptions, and misconceptions.

For these reasons it is important for a student to take a close look at the author of the data that are being considered for use. This is the purpose of the

Figure 7.3. Student ANALZYING Tool for Documenting Sources (3A5)

Project: _Beluga Whales_ **Teacher:** _Ms. Jones_ **Student(s):** _Jessica Pembroke_

1. **Web site:** _New York Aquarium_ **http://** _www.wcs.org/zoos/aquarium/aganimals/beluga.html_

   Last modified: _29 May 1999_ **Out of date?** _no, it looks very current_

   Subject: _Beluga Whales_ **Heading:** _"White Whale of the Arctic Seas"_

   Author: _unknown_ **Credentials:** _Wildlife Conservation Society_

   Employer: (self) (institution) (company) (society) (lobby) (group) (other): _Wildlife Conservation Society_

   Perspective: (pro) (neutral) (con): _celebrates and wants to conserve the belugas_

   Intended audience: (general) (schools) (adults) (special interest) (members) (consumers) (new members)
   (others): _an aquarium run by the city for the public_

2. **Web site:** _Sea World_ **http://** _www.seaworld.org/beluga_whales/befirst.html_

   Last modified: _16 Dec 1999_ **Out of date?** _no_

   Subject: _Beluga Whales_ **Heading:** _"Sea World Education Department Resource"_

   Author: _not listed_ **Credentials:** _"Sea World Education Department"_

   Employer: (self) (institution) (company) (society) (lobby) (group) (other): _Sea World, Busch Gardens_

   Perspective: (pro) (neutral) (con): _"For in the end we will conserve only what we love. We will love only what we understand. We will understand only what we are taught." -B. Dioum_

   Intended audience: (general) (schools) (adults) (special interest) (members) (consumers) (new members)
   (others): _aimed at people wanting to see sea life_

3. **Web site:** _____ **http://** _____

   Last modified: _____ **Out of date?** _____

   Subject: _____ **Heading:** _____

   Author: _____ **Credentials:** _____

   Employer: (self) (institution) (company) (society) (lobby) (group) (other): _____

   Perspective: (pro) (neutral) (con): _____

   Intended audience: (general) (schools) (adults) (special interest) (members) (consumers) (new members)
   (others): _____

Student *Analyzing* Tool for Web Sites. When a student finds what appears to be a good source for answering the student's questions, the Student *Analyzing* Tool for Documenting Sources (Figure 7.3) is used to authenticate and document the site, as shown here in the worked example. This tool is quite advanced, and students will need guidance when they use it. Initially, it is often difficult for them to determine the perspective or agenda of the writer or creator of the Web site, but with guidance and practice they can become adept at doing this for themselves.

Sometimes, a student finds a Web site that is indispensable to his or her needs, but the author's credibility cannot be established or is in some other way suspect. In this case, the author's data might be quoted on the condition that it is accompanied with a full explanation of student's reservations and suspicions. An author's credibility may be partially established by comparing the author's work against a more clearly qualified person's work. If the relatively unqualified person's work seems to be more detailed and extensive by comparison, then this should be noted. Conversely, the credibility of a supposedly well-qualified author could be called into question if sound available knowledge from other sources is known to contradict it.

Despite these nuances, the Student *Analyzing* Tool for Documenting Sources is a good start for attempting to establish the credibility of an author's work under consideration for inclusion in a student's work.

Closing Comments

The *Analyzing* Tool for Documenting Sources also belongs to the *Accessing* section. It is designed to work with the Student *Accessing* Tool. As students access information, documentation and authority can be checked on immediately.

It's important to remember that all the tools work with each and that the 5A process is, in fact, one continuous thinking event. We have tried to simplify it into its elements so that it makes instructional sense and is easier for students to learn.

Chapter 8

Stage 4: APPLYING—Teacher and Student Tools

In this chapter we introduce two tools, the Stage 4: *Applying* Lesson Planner (Figure 8.1) for teachers and the Student *Applying* Tool for Presentations (Figure 8.2). Both tools are presented as worked examples. Blank versions that can be photocopied for use are found in the Appendixes.

Stage 4: *Applying* Lesson Planner

The Stage 4: *Applying* Lesson Planner, shown in Figure 8.1, is used with the Ten-Minute Lesson Planner, described in Chapter 4, and the other four detailed Lesson Planners. The purpose of the *Applying* Lesson Planner is to help teachers integrate presentation skills into any instructional unit or project. The *Applying* Lesson Planner can be regarded as an extension of the *Applying* component of the Ten-Minute Lesson Planner, where the teacher has already identified the general *Applying* Skill Sets to be addressed during the project. By referring to the complete Skills Framework, which is located in Part III, the teacher can now use the *Applying* Planner to identify the specific *Applying* skills that are to be introduced or reinforced during the implementation of the *Applying* stage.

Figure 8.1 shows a completed version of Ms. Jones's lesson plan for implementing the *Applying* stage. The Stage 4: *Applying* Lesson Planner is structured exactly the same as the other lesson planners. The *Applying* Lesson Planner has the same five components, numbered 4A to 4E, which are designed to work with the five major components of the *Applying* Skills Framework. Structurally, each of the components in the Planner outlines the goal of the component, gives a summary of the skill sets in that component, and lists the sections related to planning the implementation of that component. The five components of the Stage 4: *Applying* Lesson Planner can be summarized as follows.

- 4A *Applying* Essential Skills: This is the central part of the tool, where the teacher uses the Skills Framework to identify which of the Essential or core *Applying* skills are going to be introduced or reinforced.

- 4B *Applying* Prerequisite Skills: Here the teacher considers which basic or foundational *Applying* skills need to be in place to complete the project and makes a note in the box on how to check up in class on any suspected skill weaknesses. If there are skills that are not found in the Framework, the teacher can add them to the *Essential* Skills component under the section entitled "Skills to be introduced."

Figure 8.1. Stage 4: APPLYING Lesson Planner

4B. Applying Prerequisite Skills

Goal: to check your assumptions about what basic Applying skills students should already have

Basic Student Skills Needed for a Presentation
1. Preparation Skills   2. Graphics Skills   3. Writing Skills
4. Technical Writing   5. Audio Skills   6. Video Skills
7. Multimedia Skills   8. General

- general presentation skills using writing
- basic computer skills

Add any basic skills that are not included in the Skills Framework to the Essential Skills section below

4C. Applying Techniques Skills

Goal: to consider the best possible methods for students to make (Apply) their presentations

Possible Methods
Student Applying Tool for Presentations
1. General   2. Graphic   3. Writing   4. Technical Writing
5. Oral   6. Debate   7. Audio   8. Video
9. Multimedia   10. Internet

- all students to hand in 1000 word typewritten report with emphasis on all student tools properly completed

4A. Applying Essential Skills

Goal: to identify the Applying skills you want students to develop during the preparation and presentation of their projects

1. Several Sources skills 2. General Presentation skills 3. Graphics skills 4. Writing skills
5. Technical Writing skills 6. Oral skills 7. Debating skills 8. Audio skills 9. Video skills
10. Multimedia skills 11. Internet skills 12. General

Skills to be introduced
- 4A4(s) Converts outline steps into correct sentences
- 4A2(h) Examines and integrates alternative points of view

Skills to be reinforced
- 4A4(a-g) Writing Presentation Skills Set

4D. Applying Equipment Needs

Goal: to make sure that the equipment needed for Applying information is available and working properly

1. Hardware needs
a. Multimedia computer b. VCR c. Video editing
d. Tape player e. Audio editing f. Photocopier
- printer attached to computer

2. Software needs
a. Drawing program b. Word processor c. Database
d. Sound editing program e. Video editing program
f. Multimedia program g. Publishing program
h. Internet publishing program

4E. Applying Reviewing Skills

Goal: to assess that the Applying processes are properly and fully implemented

1. Student Process Review

2. Collaborative Process Review

- students work in pairs/groups to review each other's work

3. Teacher Process Review

- 4C *Applying* Techniques Skills: Here the teacher considers the best possible methods for students to use in presenting the information they have accessed and analyzed.

- 4D *Applying* Equipment Needs (called "Technology Skills" in the Skills Framework): Here the teacher considers what equipment will be necessary to implement the *Applying* stage and makes a note to check that the equipment is available and working properly.

- 4E *Applying* Review Skills: Here the teacher considers how to assess the way the *Applying* stage was implemented and if the teacher's and students' goals for this stage were achieved; students should be encouraged to self-assess their own presentations immediately after they have been presented.

How Ms. Jones Uses the *Applying* Lesson Planner

Ms. Jones checks the Ten-Minute Lesson Planner for the Skill Sets that she had identified for *Applying* during her initial planning and then examines the complete Skills Framework to identify specific Essential *Applying* Skills that she wants to introduce to her students during the "whales" project. She then moves through the Prerequisite Skills, Techniques Skills, Equipment Needs, and Review Skills components to make sure that they are aligned with each other as well as the *Asking*, *Accessing*, and *Analyzing* Lesson Planners. She goes back and forth between the various components until all five seem to fit together into a single cohesive strategy.

She decides to use the Student *Applying* Tool (Figure 8.2), which she plans to give to the students in the *Asking* Stage of the project. Even though her requirements are for the students to write a 1,000-word report using a word processor, she understands that the NetSavvy process is intended to make students more aware of different means for presenting information. As her class becomes more aware of the different ways of presenting information, she plans to give them more choices based on their expanding and maturing *Applying* skill levels.

The Student *Applying* Tools

The data that a student has gathered, analyzed, and authenticated now have to be worked into the form of the presentation agreed upon at the beginning of the project. Traditionally, a project would result in a lengthy hand-written report submitted to the teacher. Today, the Internet facilitates the opportunity for a student to work with a word processor, audio files, and video files. This presents a number of new possibilities for presentations. A student can use a computer to present an illustrated essay, a slide show with recorded narration, or a work with audio and video clips to the teacher. Beyond this, the Internet provides a platform to easily publish these same materials and present them to a small, specialized group or even a potential audience of millions. If an e-mail address is included with the publication, then

Figure 8.2. Student APPLYING Tool

Project: *Whales*   **Teacher:** *Ms. Jones*   **Student(s):** *Jessica Pembroke*

(4C) Consider methods for creating a presentation

(2) Graphics: map; graph; illustration...

(3) Writing: (report) essay; journal entry
    article; short story; letter; poem...

(4) Technical writing: report; guide...

(5) Oral: speech; interview; drama...

(6) Debate: one-on-one; group...

(7) Audio: interview; speech; story; musical recital...

(8) Video: video recording; animation...

(9) Multimedia: audio; video; graphics; pictures; text

(10) Internet publishing: Web site; personal e-mail;
        listserv posting; newsgroup posting...

Notes: *1000 word report*

(4D) Consider tools for creating a presentation

(1) Hardware

(a) Multimedia computer

(b) VCR

(c) Video editing equipment

(d) Tape player

(e) Audio editing equipment

(f) Photocopier

(g) Other...

(2) Software

(a) Drawing/graphing program: _____

(b) Word processing program: *MS Word* _____

(c) Database program: _____

(d) Sound editing program: _____

(e) Video editing program: _____

(f) Multimedia program: _____

(g) Publishing program: _____

(h) Internet publishing program: _____

Notes: *will use computer at home too*

(4B) Checklist for creating a presentation

[X] Have addressed the obstacles to creating an effective presentation
      I got my new reading glasses

[X] Have edited the work for spelling, punctuation & consistency
      I got my mom to help me with this

[X] Have proofed the work for vocabulary & sentence structure

[X] Have rehearsed & checked the work for flow
      I read it out loud

[X] Have made extra effort to do an excellent job
      I ran out of time

[X] To make my presentation better I can:
      It would be a lot better with pictures in it

anyone viewing the work is in a position to provide feedback. Ultimately the Internet provides amazing open-ended possibilities for publication and feedback to build on knowledge. Although the school setting is necessarily limited in this respect, it is a great starting point, one where students can learn basics that can be enhanced with further education and experience.

For a student such as Jessica Pembroke, doing a project on whales is likely to generate interest in a range of possibilities for presenting work, particularly in light of the new capabilities presented by the Internet. This is the purpose of the *Applying* Tool for Presentations. However, this tool can also be used with data that have been accessed, analyzed, and processed by traditional methods.

The Student *Applying* Tool for Presentations

Next, let's consider the Student *Applying* Tool for Presentations, which is shown in Figure 8.2. The tool is made up of three components that summarize the possibilities described in the Skills Framework:

- A checklist for considering different ways of presenting information
- A checklist for considering different tools for creating the presentation
- A checklist for making sure that the presentation or product that is being created has undergone the proper processing in terms of formatting, spelling, proofing, and so on.

These checklists are a simple and efficient way to prompt students to consider possibilities for presentations and presentation tools. The ultimate purpose of the NetSavvy process is to make students become more responsible for their work and thinking. For this to happen, teachers need to model and teach the different NetSavvy skills and then use the process of progressive withdrawal of support to the students, thus giving them increasing responsibility for their own learning at all five stages.

During the early stages of implementation of the NetSavvy process, this tool serves to raise the level of awareness of different ways for students to present their research. Later, as students become more savvy, they can begin to make their own decisions as to how they can best present information. The work the student has done up to this fourth stage may affect the form of presentation. For example, if in the *Accessing* stage a student is able to interview an exceptional expert, it might be agreed that the student should present the dialogue of the recorded interview as the project instead of an essay on the topic as was previously agreed to. It is important to keep in mind that the ultimate goal is to have students take on as much ownership and responsibility for their work and the learning process as possible. Thus, while a teacher may prescribe the parameters of the final student presentation, given the possibilities of on-line communication and interaction, it is better to keep an open mind as to how and what the student can present.

Note: In the worked example of the Student *Applying* Tool for Presentations, the numbering of the presentation methods under heading (4C) begins with

"(2) Graphics . . ." and not "1" because these bracketed numbers indicate the exact part of the Skills Framework from which the material was copied. For example, in the NetSavvy Skills Framework 4C2 is the *Applying* Techniques Skill Sets for Graphics, and 4C3 is the *Applying* Techniques Skill Sets for Writing. On the blank version of the tool that is given to the student, the numbering is purely sequential and not directly linked to the NetSavvy Framework.

Closing Comments

Implementation of the *Applying* stage is critical to learners from two aspects. One aspect of *Applying* is that information comes in all flavors—text, video, images, and sound and in different media. Each medium has specific formats or ways of presenting information. Students need to learn how techniques, styles, and different media can bend information and skew the presentation and, therefore, our perceptions. In effect, although students need to learn how to create a variety of presentations, they also need to learn how to interpret presentations and different media. This aspect needs both *Analyzing* skills and *Applying* skills and once again, we see how the 5As are interconnected with each other and that the boundaries between them are somewhat artificial.

The second aspect has to do with learning specific *Applying* skills during the project. During this stage, students can demonstrate all the work they have done and what has been learned. The traditional presentation has been a written report or, at best, some type of slide presentation created on a computer with an audience of one—the teacher. Now, given the potential of Internet communication and interactivity, all this is changing. Virtually anyone who is qualified or interested can become the learner's audience, giving critical and timely commentary. Such feedback is crucial to enhancing further learning and expanding a student's sense of the possible.

Often, students feel that the work they do is irrelevant, meaningless, or a necessary evil to get a grade. Often, learners will rush through to get the work done (which frequently halts at the *Accessing* Stage), get their grade, and get out. This is not how true learning happens. Students must become involved and feel that what they are doing is important or relevant. Sometimes learning, particularly theoretical facts, is downright hard. This can be made easier by helping students find some relevance for the hard work that has to be done.

Thus, all students must learn how to use all five stages of the NetSavvy process to make the work relevant, meaningful, useful, and motivating. But if this is to happen, it is up to the teacher to be flexible enough to allow for the restructuring of the *Applying* stage. How teachers plan and implement the *Applying* stage will shape the other four stages of *Asking, Accessing, Analyzing,* and *Assessing.* Furthermore, by building flexibility and openness in the planning of the *Applying* stage, students can learn how to negotiate *how* and *what* they present. This can only help in motivating students to do better and learn more. After all, that is the goal.

Chapter 9

Stage 5: ASSESSING—Teacher and Student Tools

In Chapter 9, we introduce three tools, the Stage 4: *Assessing* Lesson Planner (Figure 9.1), the Student *Assessing* Tool for Presentations (Figure 9.2), and the Student *Assessing* Tool for Process Skills (Figure 9.3). Each tool is presented as a worked tool. Blank versions that can be photocopied for use are found in the Appendixes.

Stage 5: *Assessing* Lesson Planner

The Stage 5: *Assessing* Lesson Planner, shown in Figure 9.1, is used with the Ten-Minute Lesson Planner. The purpose of the *Assessing* Lesson Planner is to help teachers plan the assessing of student work and to integrate *Assessing* skills into any instructional unit or project, at any grade level. In Chapters 5 through 8, we introduced detailed Lesson Planners for the other four stages of the NetSavvy process (*Asking, Accessing, Analyzing,* and *Applying*). Remember that when developing detailed lesson plans, teachers should photocopy blank versions of all five Lesson Planners and then begin working from their completed Ten-Minute Lesson Planner.

The *Assessing* Lesson Planner can be regarded as a detailed extension of the *Assessing* component of the Ten-Minute Lesson Planner, where the teacher has already identified the general *Assessing* Skill Sets to be addressed during the project. By referring to the complete Skills Framework, which is located in Part III, the teacher can now use the *Assessing* Planner to identify the specific *Assessing* skills that are to be introduced or reinforced during the implementation of the *Assessing* stage.

Figure 9.1 shows a completed version of Ms. Jones' lesson plan for implementing the *Assessing* stage. The Stage 5: *Assessing* Lesson Planner is structured exactly the same as the other lesson planners. The *Assessing* Lesson Planner has the same five components, numbered 5A to 5E, which are designed to work with the five major components of the *Assessing* Skills Framework. Structurally, each of the components in the Planner outlines the goal of the component, gives a summary of the Skill Sets in that component, and lists the sections related to planning the implementation of that component. The five components of the Stage 4: *Assessing* Lesson Planner can be summarized as follows.

- 5A *Assessing* Essential Skills: This is the central part of the tool, where the teacher uses the Skills Framework to identify which of the Essential or core *Assessing* skills are going to be introduced or reinforced.

Figure 9.1. Stage 5: ASSESSING Lesson Planner

5B. Assessing Prerequisite Skills

Goal: to check your assumptions about what basic Assessing skills students should already have

Basic Student Skills Needed for Being Assessed

- *5B1(c) Understands the nature of the learning process*
- *emphasize to students the importance of process as well as content*

Add any basic skills that are not included in the Skills Framework to the Essential Skills section below

5C. Assessing Techniques Skills

Goal: to consider the best possible methods of Assessing student processes and presentations

Possible Methods

1. Presentation Assessing Methods
Student Assessing Tool for Presentations
a. Teacher b. Student c. Peers d. Collaborators
e. Live audience f. Internet audience g. Other

2. Process Assessing Methods
Student Assessing Tool for Process Skills
a. Teacher b. Student c. Peers d. Collaborators
e. Live audience f. Internet audience g. Other

5A. Assessing Essential Skills

Goal: to identify the skills you want students to develop during the Assessing stage

1. Student Self-Assessing Skills 2. Tool Assessing Skills 3. Process Assessing Skills
4. Technique Assessing Skills 5. Technology Assessing Skills
6. Transfer of Learning

Skills to be introduced
- *5A5 Transfer of Learning Skill Set*
- *make connection to personal life experiences and recent visit to the Aquarium*

Skills to be reinforced

- *5B1(a) Appreciate the value of an outsider's point of view*
- *5B1(d) Appreciate the value of the process as much as the outcome*

5D. Assessing Equipment Needs

Goal: to make sure that the equipment or material needed for Assessing is ready

1. Presentation Assessing Tools
a. Written (test, letter grade, percent, checklist, notes, live audience questionnaire, Internet audience...)
b. Verbal (questions, comments, voting by teachers, collaborators, peers, audience...)
c. Contemplative (student self-assessment)
- *photocopy student Assessing tools for distribution*

2. Process Assessing Tools
a. Written (checklist notes, survey...)
b. Verbal (questions, comments by teachers, peers...)
c. Contemplative (student self-assessment)
- *photocopy student Assessing tools for distribution*

5E. Assessing Reviewing Skills

Goal: to check that the Assessing processes are fully and properly implemented

1. Teacher Review of Assessing
a. Teacher review of student assessing work
b. Teacher review of assessing goals and results
- *collect student presentation and process tools for evaluation*

2. Project Review by Others
a. Student review of overall project
b. Others review of overall project
- *talk to Janine about being the outside reviewer*

- 5B *Assessing* Prerequisite Skills: Here the teacher considers which basic or foundational *Assessing* skills need to be in place to assess the project and the process and makes a note in the box on how to check up in class on any suspected skill weaknesses; if there are skills that are not found in the Framework, the teacher can add them to the Essential Skills component under the section entitled "Skills to be introduced."

- 5C *Assessing* Techniques Skills: Here the teacher considers the best possible methods for assessing students' presentations and the development of their process skills.

- 5D *Assessing* Equipment Needs (called "Technology Skills" in the Skills Framework): Here the teacher considers what equipment will be necessary to implement the *Assessing* stage and makes a note to check that the tools and materials such as presentation assessing tools or process assessing tools are ready.

- 5E *Assessing* Review Skills: Here the teacher considers how to assess the way the *Assessing* stage was implemented and if the teacher's and students' goals for this stage were achieved. The teacher can make notes on how both the project and process used to complete it will be reviewed.

How Ms. Jones Uses the *Assessing* Lesson Planner

Ms. Jones consults the Ten-Minute Lesson Planner for the Skill Sets that she had identified for *Assessing* during her initial planning and then examines the complete Skills Framework to identify specific Essential *Assessing* Skills that she wants to introduce to her students as she wraps up the "whales" project. She then moves through the Prerequisite Skills, Techniques Skills, Technology Skills, and Review Skills components to make sure that they are aligned with each other as well as the *Asking, Accessing, Analyzing*, and *Applying* Lesson Planners. She goes back and forth between the various components until all five seem to fit together into a single cohesive strategy.

The Student *Assessing* Tools

Assessing occurs at several levels and starts early in the 5A NetSavvy process. At the first stage, an understanding is developed as to what is expected in terms of student learning. The *Assessing* stage is closely knitted with the *Applying* stage since assessment is done when the project is complete and a presentation is made (or a product is generated). Both application and assessment involve communication between the student's work and the student's audience. Students present their work to an audience that provides feedback on the presentation. The student could present work in the form of an essay to a teacher for marking; as a speech to the entire community, who may respond with applause, questions, and comments; or on the Internet for a specialized audience, who are invited to respond by e-mail.

The Student *Assessing* Tool for Presentations

The purpose of the Student *Assessing* Tool for Presentations (Figure 9.2) is to establish and agree upon what form a presentation may or will take. The three basic sections of the tool are summarized as follows:

- Considering methods for assessing a presentation
- Considering tools for assessing a presentation
- Self-assessment questionnaire

The first and second sections of the Student *Assessing* Tool for Presentations help to identify for the student and teacher possible methods for assessing the student's presentation. The assessment choices made using this form should have been carefully considered at the beginning of the process and then possibly reviewed and revised at some point or points along the way. Certainly if a student uncovers unexpectedly good data in the *Accessing* stage, they may want to negotiate delivering a more involved presentation or simply a different one.

The third section of the Student *Assessing* Tool for Presentations is used as a checklist and reflective tool so students can assess their own work at the conclusion of the project. However, since the students are introduced to the tool at the start of the project, the tool can also serve as an ongoing point of reference for assessing their experiences *during* the project.

The second tool presented in this section is the Student *Assessing* Tool for Process Skills (Figure 9.3). For each project or instructional unit the teacher develops a unique version of this tool. The teacher uses the Stage 1 to 5 *Asking, Accessing, Analyzing, Applying*, and *Assessing* Lesson Planners to create a rubric of all of the skills that he or she intends to introduce and/or reinforce during the project. This rubric is presented to the student at the beginning of a project, so students can assess their current level of understanding of these skills. Once the project is over, the same tool can be given back to the student so they can reassess their understanding. This provides both the students and the teacher with a snapshot of how much learning has actually occurred during a project, as well as what still needs to be improved.

In the Industrial Age, a student's report on whales would normally be marked entirely on the content and presentation. In the Information and Communication Age, although content is still important, equal value is given to the acquisition of the process skills used to complete the project. Revisiting each stage of the process to consider what worked, what didn't, what skills were learned, how they were learned, and what skills still need to be improved is critical to the NetSavvy process for *both* the teacher and the student.

In Summary

In Part II we introduced tools for teachers and students to help teach the NetSavvy 5As process. Each of the tools is designed to work with data retrieved from the

Figure 9.2. Student ASSESSING Tool for Presentations

Project: *Whales*   **Teacher:** *Ms. Jones*   **Student(s):** *Jessica*

(5C) Assessing **Methods**—fill in with teacher at start of project

(5C1) Considering Presentation Assessing Methods

(a) Teacher assessment (b) Student self-assessment (c) Peer assessment (d). Collaborator assessment
(e) Live audience assessement (f) Internet audience assessment (g) Student, parent or teacher
   assessment of possible transfer of learning to job, to other school subjects, to self, to the future...

Notes: *a: 1000 word report to be marked out of 100   b: I'll get my best friend to read it*
      c: My parents will want to read my report

(5D) Assessing **Tools**—fill in with teacher at start of project

(5D1) Considering Presentation Assessing Tools

(a) Written assessment tools: mark; test; letter grade; percentage; checklist; notes; live
   audience questionnaire; e-mail; Internet audience response...

Notes:

(b) Verbal assessment tools: questions; comments; applause; voting...

Notes:

(c) Contemplative self-assessment tools: questions; mark; notes; checklist; questionnaire—
   a sample is provided below...

Notes:

(5A1) Presentation Self-Assessment Questionnaire—do just after presentation

(a) What were my goals?
   To do a good job and get a good mark

(b) How were my goals achieved?
   I worked hard and thought I did a pretty good job

(c) What new knowledge have I learned?
   Belugas are smart and in some way, a lot like us, I think!

(d) What new skills have I learned?
   I now know how to use the Internet to find aquariums

(f) What impact has my work had on me?
   I know how to look for information from more than one source

(k) What should be done differently in the future?
   Picking which web sites to use

(m) What was the most difficult & why?
   Picking which web sites to use

(n) What was least enjoyed & why?
   Waiting to use the computer to do my report

(o) What was most enjoyed & why?
   Talking about whales in class and I got to tell my class what I know

Other comments:

Figure 9.3. Student ASSESSING Tool for Process Skills

Project: *Whales*   **Teacher:** *Ms. Jones*   **Student(s):** *Jessica Pembroke*

Instructions: Read each of the process skills and then circle the number 3, 2, 1 or 0 for that skill based on how you assess yourself in that particular skill. For example, look at 1.Asking, skill 1C1a (Can create idea map)—if you are getting the skill but need more practice, you would circle "2." The number of skills rated multiplied by 3 equals the maximum possible score.

Key

3 = I get it and feel I have a good handle on this skill
2 = I am getting it, but I really could do with some more practice
1 = I don't really get it and could do with some help
0 = This is a new topic. I don't understand what this is and need some help

Process skills

	Before project	After project
1. Asking		
(1C1a) Can create idea map	(0) 1 2 3	0 1 (2) 3
(1B1a) See the teacher privately when I have problems	0 1 (2) 3	0 1 2 (3)
(1A3b) Can tell stories from personal experiences, movies, stories I have read	0 (1) 2 3	0 1 (2) 3
(1A3a) Can ask questions which focus on new areas of knowledge & application	(0) 1 2 3	0 (1) 2 3
(1A3e) Can ask hypothetical questions of experiences	0 (1) 2 3	0 1 2 (3)
2. Accessing		
(2A2b) Know how to get on the Internet	0 1 (2) 3	0 1 2 (3)
(2A2f) Know how to use a search engine using different signs	0 (1) 2 3	0 1 (2) 3
(2C2) Know the difference between directories & indexing search engines	0 (1) 2 3	0 1 (2) 3
(2A2a) Understand how to use Netiquette & have good manners	(0) 1 2 3	0 1 2 (3)
(2C4) Know how to get to first-hand information	0 (1) 2 3	0 1 (2) 3
3. Analyzing		
(3A1e) Know how to look for differences between different sources of info	0 (1) 2 3	0 (1) 2 3
(3A1f) Understand & can spot different points of view	0 (1) 2 3	0 1 2 (3)
(3B1d) Can sift through good & bad information	0 (1) 2 3	0 (1) 2 3
(3B2d) Can see if the information is relevant or not	(0) 1 2 3	0 (1) 2 3
4. Applying		
(4A4s) Can convert outline steps into correct sentences	0 (1) 2 3	0 1 (2) 3
(4B2h) Can examine & integrate alternative points of view	0 (1) 2 3	0 1 (2) 3
(4A4f) Can proofread text for grammatical structure, punctuation, structure	0 (1) 2 3	0 1 (2) 3
5. Assessing		
(5B1a) Appreciates the value of an outsider's point of view	(0) 1 2 3	0 (1) 2 3
(5B1d) Appreciates the value of the process as much as the outcome	(0) 1 2 3	0 (1) 2 3

	Total before	Total after
maximum possible score is number of skills X 3: *19* X 3 = *57*	*15* ,57	*37* ,57

Internet. However, all the tools may be adapted and restructured for use with traditionally retrieved paper-based data. You may want to customize the tools that we have introduced in Part II to suit your own needs. In doing this, be certain to remember that we have aligned the tools structurally and functionally to the Skills Framework.

Now let's turn our attention to Part III of the book, the NetSavvy Skills Framework. The Skills Framework is the structural organizer of the many skills that we feel are essential to becoming NetSavvy and InfoSavvy. Beyond this, it is also crucial that the entire 5As process be included. Traditionally, there is a tendency to stop after the *Accessing* stage. Once students access information, we quickly move them through simple ways of *Applying* the data in the form of a content test, a report, an essay, or even an electronic presentation. The NetSavvy 5As process asks us to go a little deeper into what is being learned, while at the same time being so simple to do that the steps of the process can be counted on one hand. Understanding the NetSavvy process shows us that we are only five steps away from solving any information need or problem.

Part III

The NetSavvy Skills Framework

The NetSavvy Skills Framework is a compilation of the skills needed for using the Internet to address information needs. It is the basis for teachers to use project-based learning to embed Internet skills in any subject and at any grade level. From a teacher's point of view, the Framework serves as a set of instructions on the how and what of teaching Internet skills, and the Teacher Tools serve as a step-by-step guide in how to use the Framework to this end. From a student's point of view, the Framework is a straight listing of the skills that should be learned to achieve information literacy in the use of the Internet. The Student Tools guide the student in developing Internet skills in the course of doing a project.

Summary of the 5As of Information Literacy

The 5As of Information Literacy comprise a five-stage process for addressing any information need:

Stage 1: *Asking* (key questions to be answered)

Stage 2: *Accessing* (relevant data)

Stage 3: *Analyzing* (the acquired data)

Stage 4: *Applying* (the data to the task)

Stage 5: *Assessing* (both the end result and the process)

Summary of the Uses of the NetSavvy Skills Framework

The Skills Framework is organized in a way that is intimately tied to the 5As process of information literacy. The focus at each stage is on the "A. Essential Skills," which are the skills required to implement each stage. At the same time, consideration must also be given to "B. Prerequisite Skills." These are the basic skills the teacher assumes the students already have. The "C. Techniques Skills" are the methods used to implement the skills. The "D. Technology Skills" are the equipment needs for the project, and "E. Review Skills" represent the process of assessing how well each of the stages is learned and implemented. Consequently the headings in the Skills Framework look like this:

Stage 1: *Asking*	**Stage 2:** *Accessing*
A. *Asking* Essential Skill Sets	A. *Accessing* Essential Skill Sets
B. *Asking* Prerequisite Skill Sets	B. *Accessing* Prerequisite Skill Sets
C. *Asking* Techniques Skill Sets	C. *Accessing* Techniques Skill Sets
D. *Asking* Technology Skill Sets	D. *Accessing* Technology Skill Sets
E. *Asking* Review Skill Sets	E. *Accessing* Review Skill Sets

Stage 3... and so on

Taking a Closer Look at the Layout of the Skills Framework

Some teachers may just want to scan the Framework for ideas to use on their own terms in a single lesson. We recommend starting with the Ten-Minute Lesson Planner, whether the intent is to teach a single lesson or to lay out a quick overview of a large project. The layout of the Framework is a helpful guide for the lesson-planning process, particularly when a teacher is organizing the details of a student project. Once the teacher has first used the Framework to complete the Ten-Minute Lesson Planner, the next step is to make photocopies of the five Teacher Tools that correspond to using the five stages of the NetSavvy process and to make sample copies of the Student Tools.

The teacher now has all that is needed to proceed. The content objectives that were listed in the Ten-Minute Lesson Planner and the assessment objectives that were identified should be kept in mind. Turning to the Framework, the Essential Skill Sets (A) can be used as a checklist to get a sense of the information literacy skills that students already have and the extent to which these skills have been mastered. The remaining skills in the Essential Skill Sets represent the skills the students do not have or that need to be reinforced. The teacher can then consider introducing these skills into the learning activities of the project. The Prerequisite Skill Sets (B) should be consulted to quickly check that students have the prerequisite skills needed to complete the project. If the teacher suspects the students' skills are weak in an area, this will have to be confirmed in class by questioning or testing. The Techniques Skill Sets (C) help the teacher and students to consider the different methods that could be used to work through each stage of the 5As process. The Technology Skill Sets (D) identify possible technologies and technology skills that students could use to complete the project and the equipment that teachers will have made sure is available. The Review Skill Sets (E) are used to consider how teachers and students can review and reflect on whether their goals have been met at each stage of the NetSavvy process.

The Skills Framework Symbols

There are a number of variables in any given teaching situation that can greatly affect instructional strategies and outcomes. Issues such as learning styles, skill levels, prior experience, and knowledge can have a great impact on when and how skills can be most effectively introduced. The exact grade levels when information literacy skills for NetSavvy should be taught will depend to a great extent upon the abilities of your students, your instructional and learning objectives, and the time frames in which you are working. With this in mind and based on field testing, we have tried to approximate the grade levels at which the skills may be most appropriately introduced, mastered, and reinforced.

The symbols E, M, and R are used in the Skills Framework to suggest that level of understanding of the skill appropriate to the grade level (as shown in the key below).

Key:

E = Emerging

M = Mastering

R = Reinforcing

The first level, E, is an introductory or emergent stage in the development of the skill, in which the teacher is most heavily involved. The second level, M, indicates that students understand the skills and can apply that understanding with some assistance from the teacher. At the third level, R, students can perform the skills on their own and can engage in activities to maintain and extend the understanding.

The symbols P, I, M, H, and + indicate the grade levels within which the different skills are best introduced, mastered, or reinforced.

Key:

P represents Primary or grades K–2

I represents Intermediate or grades 3–5

M represents Middle School or grades 6–9

H represents High School or grades 10–12

+ represents Postsecondary level

**A
S
K
I
N
G**

Stage 1: *Asking*

Skills for Preparing Questions

The *Asking* stage is the key to engaging students in the learning process. The teacher introduces a topic and guides the students to generate their own questions related to that topic. This more clearly defines the boundaries for research. Questions posed by students and teachers clarify the information needs and define possible paths for inquiry using the Internet, as well as other electronic or traditional paper-based sources.

E = Emerging, M = Mastering, R = Reinforcing, P = Primary (gr. K–2), I = Intermediate (gr. 3–5), M = Middle School (gr. 6–9), H = High School (gr. 10–12), + = Postsecondary

1A. *Asking* Essential Skill Sets	P	I	M	H	+
1. Critical Conversing Skill Set—Observing & Questioning					
a. Questions whether what an individual says is contradicted by their actions (congruent/incongruent behavior)			E	E	M
b. Questions whether what an individual says is contradicted by their nonverbal messages (congruent/incongruent behavior)			E	E	M
2. Critical Conversing Skill Set—Listening & Questioning					
a. Analyzes speakers' purpose (information, rapport, influence, sales…) to develop responsive questions		E	M	R	
b. Interprets speakers' perspective (objective, subjective, self-serving…) to develop responsive questions			E	M	R
c. Identifies speakers' persuasive techniques (promises, challenges, flattery…) to develop responsive questions			E	M	R
d. Distinguishes between speakers' opinion and verifiable fact to develop responsive questions			E	M	R
e. Interprets subtle verbal messages (sarcasm, exaggeration, double meanings, innuendo) to develop responsive questions		E	E	M	R

E = Emerging, M = Mastering, R = Reinforcing, P = Primary (gr. K–2), I = Intermediate (gr. 3–5), M = Middle School (gr. 6–9), H = High School (gr. 10–12), + = Postsecondary

3. Critical Conversing Skill Set—Thinking & Questioning	**P**	**I**	**M**	**H**	**+**
a. Asks questions which focus on new areas of knowledge and application		E	E	M	R
b. Uses personal interpretations of experiences, stories, poems, plays, or movies to generate questions	E	E	M	R	
c. Asks follow-up questions related to resources, obstacles, goals, possibilities...)		E	M	R	
d. Asks probing clarifying questions derived from answers received		E	M	R	
e. Asks hypothetical questions for exploring possibilities and testing relationships (what might happen if...?)		E	M	R	
f. Asks questions related to essential life questions (purpose, identity, integrity, courage, invention, inspiration, faith, life, death...)	E	E	E	M	R
g. Conveys subtle verbal and nonverbal messages while posing questions			E	M	R
1B. *Asking* Prerequisite Skill Sets	**P**	**I**	**M**	**H**	**+**
1. General Observing Skill Set					
a. Addresses personal barriers to effective observing (visual impairment, color blindness, light sensitivity...)		E	E	M	R
b. Addresses external barriers to effective observing (visual distractions, lighting, physical obstacles...)	E	M	R		
c. Interprets and evaluates speakers' facial expressions		E	M	R	
d. Interprets and evaluates speakers' gestures and body language		E	M	R	
2. General Listening Skill Set					
a. Addresses personal barriers to effective listening (hearing problems...)		E	E	M	R
b. Addresses external barriers to effective listening (noise, visual distractions...)	E	M	R		
c. Determines the purpose for listening (advice, opinions, solutions, facts, anecdotes, rapport...)		E	M	R	
d. Responds to tone of voice appropriately	E	M	R		
e. Responds to directions and questions	E	M	R		
f. Listens attentively to oral presentations (information, stories, opinion, advice...)	E	M	R		
3. General Speaking Skill Set					
a. Addresses personal barriers to effective speaking (speech impediments...)		E	E	M	R
b. Addresses external barriers to effective speaking (noise, visual distractions...)	E	M	R		
c. Responds verbally to tone of voice	E	M	R		
d. Responds verbally to directions and questions	E	M	R		
e. Determines purpose for speaking (advice, opinions, solutions, facts, story...)	E	E	M	R	

ASKING

E = Emerging, M = Mastering, R = Reinforcing, P = Primary (gr. K–2), I = Intermediate (gr. 3–5), M = Middle School (gr. 6–9), H = High School (gr. 10–12), + = Postsecondary

1C. *Asking* Techniques Skill Sets	P	I	M	H	+
1. Brainstorming Skill Set					
a. Creates idea maps		E	E	M/R	R
b. Employs brainstorming, clustering, and webbing techniques individually or cooperatively to develop questions	E	E	M	R	
2. Question-Forming Skill Set	P	I	M	H	+
a. Considers which groups or individuals may have done best work on subject		E	M	R	
b. Considers which media are likely to be the best sources for data on subject		E	M	R	
c. Considers how the topic relates to essential life questions (purpose, identity, integrity, courage, invention, inspiration, faith, life, death...)	E	E	E	M	R
d. Considers follow-up questions related to goals, resources, obstacles...)	E	E	M	R	
e. Considers hypothetical questions for exploring future possibilities and testing possible relationships or scenarios (what might happen if ...?)	E	E	M	R	
f. Uses personal strategies for selecting, developing, and refining a topic		E	E	M/R	R
g. Considers the topic at some point in the past (before you were born, pre-1900, pre-1492, pre-human contact...)		E	E	M/R	R
h. Considers the topic at some point in the future (10 years, 100 years, 1000 years)		E	E	M/R	R
3. General Conversing Skill Set					
a. Addresses barriers to effective conversing (speech problems, shyness, ESL...)		E	M	M/R	R
b. Determines the purpose for conversing (seeking advice, opinion, solutions, facts, anecdotes, rapport...)			E	M/R	R
c. Uses appropriate rate, volume, pitch, tone for the audience and setting	E	E	E	M/R	R
d. Adapts word choice, diction, and usage to the audience, purpose, and occasion	E	E	E	M/R	R
e. Uses nonverbal gestures (giving directions, introductions, making announcements...)	E	E	E	M/R	R

E = Emerging, M = Mastering, R = Reinforcing, P = Primary (gr. K–2), I = Intermediate (gr. 3–5), M = Middle School (gr. 6–9), H = High School (gr. 10–12), + = Postsecondary

4. Critical Conversing Skill Set	P	I	M	H	+
a. Determines what is already known and what needs to be known		E	E	M/R	R
b. Assesses the current knowledge base on the topic		E	E	M/R	R
c. Analyzes preconceived ideas and biases related to the topic (personal and others)		E	E	M/R	R
d. Consults with others to get ideas for questions to be asked		E	E	M/R	R
e. Determines what additional general and specific information is needed	E	E	E	M/R	R
f. Clarifies spoken messages using props (objects, pictures, charts, diagrams...)	E	E	E	M/R	R
g. Connects experiences, feelings, and ideas with others to establish rapport	E	E	E	M/R	R
h. Conveys messages nonverbally (gestures, facial expressions, body language...)		E	E	M/R	R
i. Questions an assignment's requirements in terms of personal interest		E	E	M/R	R
j. Questions the limitations of an assignment		E	E	M/R	R
k. Determines if the extent of student's knowledge on topic has been reached		E	E	M/R	R
l. Determines if the extent of teacher's knowledge on the topic has been reached		E	E	M/R	R

1D. *Asking* Technology Skill Sets

1. Computer Software Skill Set	P	I	M	H	+
a. Uses word processor for formulating questions		E	E	E	M/R
b. Uses Internet search engines to do research in preparation for formulating questions		E	E	E	M/R
c. Uses idea and concept mapping programs for brainstorming questions (Inspiration, CMap, LifeMap, Model-It...)			E	E	M/R
d. Uses CD ROM to do research in preparation for formulating questions		E	E	E	M/R
e. Considers other useful software tools for forming questions		E	E	E	M/R

2. Computer Hardware Skill Set	P	I	M	H	+
a. Uses computer for word processing or idea and concept mapping (see 2B1 2B2)		E	E	E	M/R

ASKING

E = Emerging, M = Mastering, R = Reinforcing, P = Primary (gr. K–2), I = Intermediate (gr. 3–5), M = Middle School (gr. 6–9), H = High School (gr. 10–12), + = Postsecondary

1E. *Asking* Review Skill Sets	P	I	M	H	+
1. Student Process Review Skill Set					
a. Reviews process by comparing progress to date with initial goals	E	M	R		
b. Revisits original topic and develops follow-up questions			E	M	R
c. Uses existing data to further clarify the boundaries of the topic			E	M	R
d. Revisits original instructions to determine if scope of task was fully explored		E	M	R	
2. Collaborative Process Review Skill Set					
a. Works with others (peers, teacher, family) to review process by comparing progress to date with initial goals	E	M	R		
b. Works with others to revisit original topic and develops follow-up questions			E	M	R
c. Works with others in using existing data to further clarify boundaries of topic			E	M	R
d. Works with others to revisit original instructions to determine if scope of task was fully explored		E	M	R	
e. Uses self-assessment and collaborative Skill Set to determine if topic is practical		E	E	M	R
3. Teacher Process Review					
a. Review of teacher's *Asking* goals and results					

Stage 2: *Accessing*

Skills for Accessing Data from the Internet and Other Sources

In the *Accessing* stage, students engage in the data-collection component of the NetSavvy process. Now that the assignment is understood, the initial questions have been defined, and the research boundaries have been narrowed, the time for considering possible data sources and how to access them is at hand.

E = Emerging, M = Mastering, R = Reinforcing, P = Primary (gr. K–2), I = Intermediate (gr. 3–5), M = Middle School (gr. 6–9), H = High School (gr. 10–12), + = Postsecondary

2A. *Accessing* Essential Skill Sets	P	I	M	H	+
1. Skill Set for Using Hardware					
a. Computer skills for word processing, Internet browsing, e-mail, and recording, arranging, and modifying data	E	E	E	E/M	R
b. Data management skills for storing and backing-up data and software to storage devices (disks, hard drive, Zip drive, optical drive...)	E	E	E	E/M	R
c. CD ROM search skills for accessing data	E	E	M	R	
d. Multimedia computer skills for accessing, viewing, and manipulating pictures, animation, and motion video		E	E	E/M	R
e. Network skills for accessing data from local area networks (LANs)	E	E	M	R	
f. Modem skills for configuring the modem and connecting to the Internet		E	E	E/M	R
g. Scanner skills for scanning photographs and graphics		E	E	M	R
h. VCR skills for recording and playing		E	M	R	
i. Photographic camera (film, digital) operation skills	E	E	E/M	M	R
j. Tape recorder skills for recording and playing	E	E	M	R	
k. Video camera (VHS, digital) skills for recording and playing	E	E	M	M/R	

E = Emerging, M = Mastering, R = Reinforcing, P = Primary (gr. K–2), I = Intermediate (gr. 3–5), M = Middle School (gr. 6–9), H = High School (gr. 10–12), + = Postsecondary

2. Skill Set for Using Computer Software (See Figure 6.2)	P	I	M	H	+
a. Netiquette awareness for appropriate behavior when using the Internet		E	E	M/R	R
b. Internet browser skills for navigating the Internet, entering and using URLs, and using hypertext links to locate and download data		E	E	M/R	R
c. E-mail skills for opening, reading, composing, spell-checking, attaching documents, and sending messages		E	E	M/R	R
d. Listserv skills for participating in group discussions by e-mail		E	E	E/M	R
e. Word processing skills for entering text, spell-checking, grammar-checking, using fonts and styles	E	E	E/M	R	
f. Internet search engine skills for reading search tips: simple searching, Boolean searching, searching by date range, domain, geography, language		E	E	M	R
g. Skills for using multisearch Internet engines		E	E	M	R
h. Skills for using on-line databases (setting up the account, signing on, signing off, simple searching, Boolean searching, searching by date range, domain, geography, language...)			E	E	M
i. Database program skills for organizing and recording data	E	E	E	M	R
j. Spreadsheet program skills for arranging and recording data	E	E	E	M	R
k. Skills for accessing software/hardware help files and tutorials		E	M/R		
l. Scanning skills for digitizing photos and graphics		E	E	M	R
m. Voice recognition software skills for recording the spoken word			E	E/M	R
n. Optical character recognition (OCR) program skills for digitizing text		E	E/M	R	
3. Recording Data and Creating a Bibliography					
a. Identifies appropriate tools for recording data (pen, photocopier, scanner, tape recorder, video camera, computer files...)	E	E	E	M	R
b. Identifies what should be recorded (main ideas, key statements, quotes...)		E	E	M	R
c. Organizes records (paper or electronic) of data obtained		E	E	M	R
d. Identifies bibliographic formats (APA, MLA, Internet...)		E	E	M	R
e. Creates a bibliography		E	E	M	R
f. Understands related technology skills (creating headers, footers, page breaks, footnotes...)		E	E	M	R

ACCESSING

E = Emerging, M = Mastering, R = Reinforcing, P = Primary (gr. K–2), I = Intermediate (gr. 3–5), M = Middle School (gr. 6–9), H = High School (gr. 10–12), + = Postsecondary

2B. *Accessing* Prerequisite Skill Sets	P	I	M	H	+
1. General Workstation Skill Set					
a. Adjusts chair for comfort	E	M/R			
b. Ensures that the keyboard is at the proper height	E	M/R			
c. Adjusts the image size for comfortable viewing (see under the "View" menu)	E	M/R			
d. Adjusts the monitor controls for contrast, brightness, and resolution	E	M/R			
e. Creates working space for materials and note-taking	E	M	R		
2. General Computer Skill Set					
a. Has basic working knowledge of computers (start, shut down, use mouse, open file, create new file, save file to disk, hard drive, and network)	E	M	R		
b. Keyboards at rate at least equal to handwriting rate		E	M/R		
c. Has working knowledge of word processing software commands (enter, delete, insert, cut, copy and paste, save, save as, find and replace...)		E	M	R	
3. General Internet Skill Set					
a. Has basic working knowledge of e-mail software commands (retrieve, open, save, reply, forward, queue, delete...)		E	M	R	
b. Understands basic steps of composing, addressing, and sending e-mail		E	M	R	
c. Has basic working knowledge of Internet browser software (open browser, enter URL, use tool bar, hyperlinks and bookmarks ...)		E	M	R	
d. Understands basic steps of using a search engine (identifies and enters keywords, uses hyperlinks, saves sites using bookmarks...)		E	M	R	
e. Treats equipment and disks with respect	E	M	R		
f. Respects privacy of other students' files	E	M	R		
g. Understands and respects copyright issues	E	M	R		

ACCESSING

E = Emerging, M = Mastering, R = Reinforcing, P = Primary (gr. K–2), I = Intermediate (gr. 3–5), M = Middle School (gr. 6–9),
H = High School (gr. 10–12), + = Postsecondary

4. Internet On-Line Skill Set	P	I	M	H	+
a. Demonstrates appropriate on-line behavior (is polite, uses appropriate language, does not reveal or request personal information or act in a disruptive manner)		E	M	R	
b. Respects intellectual property of other users and information providers		E	M	R	
c. Communicates with teacher regarding concerns or questionable activities		E	M	R	
5. General Reading Skill Set					
a. Addresses barriers to effective reading (eyesight, learning problems, lighting...)	E	E	E	M	R
b. Demonstrates word skills (vocabulary, word attack...)	E	E	E	M	R
c. Reads for different purposes (comprehension, appreciation, research...)		E	E	M	R
d. Reads variety of texts (nonfiction, novels, textbooks, newspapers, magazines...)		E	E	M	R
6. Technical Reading Skill Set					
a. Differentiates between reading technical and nontechnical data		E	E	M	R
b. Understands the difference in the language used in technical and nontechnical documents		E	E	M/R	
c. Understands the difference between the objectives of technical and nontechnical documents		E	E	M	R
d. Understands directional words (left, right, up, down, in, out...)	E	E	M	R	
e. Understands instructional words (locate, find, summarize...)	E	E	M	R	
f. Understands action words (turn, open, close, push...)	E	E	M	R	
g. Is familiar with technical terms (card, cable, controller, disk...)		E	E	M	R
h. Varies reading rate appropriate to the task (reading word by word for information rather than skimming)		E	E	E	M/R
i. Varies reading rate appropriate to complexity of text		E	E	E	M/R
j. Understands the necessity of reading technical material sequentially		E	M	R	
k. Interprets technical illustrations (diagrams, maps, charts, graphs...)		E	E	M/R	
l. Visualizes tasks by converting words to pictures, sounds, and actions		E	E	E	M/R
m. Visualizes end product or outcome		E	E	E/M	R
n. Identifies and resolves what hasn't been understood		E	M	R	
o. Obtains outside help when necessary		E	M	R	

E = Emerging, M = Mastering, R = Reinforcing, P = Primary (gr. K–2), I = Intermediate (gr. 3–5), M = Middle School (gr. 6–9), H = High School (gr. 10–12), + = Postsecondary

2C. *Accessing* Techniques Skill Sets	P	I	M	H	+
1. Starting Point Skill Set					
a. Lists likely data sources		E	E	E/M	R
b. Considers sources that provide alternate points of view		E	E	E	M/R
c. Employs brainstorming, clustering, and webbing techniques independently and cooperatively to identify key words		E	E	E/M	R
d. Creates list of key words to use in scanning indexes and tables of contents for material relevant to topic		E	E	E/M	R
2. Considering Possible Internet Indexing Systems					
a. Internet search engines (AltaVista, Excite, Fast, Infoseek, Inktomi Northern Light, WebCrawler...) for keyword searches		E	E	M	R
b. Internet multisearch engines (Dogpile, Metacrawler, Go2Net, Sherlock ...)		E	E	M	R
c. Internet Directories (Yahoo, Snap, Open Directory, Lycos...)					
d. Question answering search engines (Ask Jeeves, Disney Internet Guide, Yahooligans...)		E	E	E/M	R
e. Internet databases (ERIC, DIALOG, Amazon.com, Yellowpages.com...)			E	E/M	R
f. Search engines needed to access audio files (RealPlayer...)		E	E	M	R
g. Search programs needed to access video files (RealPlayer...)		E	E	M	R
h. Considers using on-line services (AOL, CompuServe, MSN...)		E	E	M	R
3. Considering Possible Data Sources by Location					
a. Classroom resources (teacher, other students, text books, Internet...)		E	E	M/R	
b. School resources (library, Internet, other teachers, district resource center...)		E	E	M/R	
c. Home resources (books, computer, Internet, parents, relatives, neighbors...)	E	E	E	M/R	
d. Community resources (libraries, Internet sites, museums, science centers, archives, galleries, local government, societies, businesses...)			E	E	M/R
e. State resources (libraries, Internet sites, museums, science centers, archives, galleries, state government, societies, businesses...)			E	E	M/R
f. Federal resources (libraries, Internet sites, museums, archives, government, businesses...)			E	E	M/R
g. International resources (foreign governments, United Nations, businesses, cultural, historical...)			E	E	M/R

A
C
C
E
S
S
I
N
G

E = Emerging, M = Mastering, R = Reinforcing, P = Primary (gr. K–2), I = Intermediate (gr. 3–5), M = Middle School (gr. 6–9), H = High School (gr. 10–12), + = Postsecondary

	P	I	M	H	+
4. Considering Possible Tools for Locating People (Primary Sources) on the Internet					
a. E-mail programs (Eudora, Messenger, Outlook Express...)		E	M	R	
b. Listservs (discussion groups by email).		E	E	M/R	
c. Internet search engines (AltaVista, Excite, Infoseek, Lycos, Northern Light, Yahoo...)		E	E	M	R
d. Newsgroups		E	E	M	R
5. Considering Possible Tools for Interacting with People in Real Time Over the Internet					
a. Discussion groups (real time), e.g., microsoft.public.win2000.*		E	E	M	R
b. Chat rooms (e.g., Collecting-Sports, FoodTalk, ePoet, Music-Jazz...)		E	E	M	R
c. MUDs (multiuser domains) (TrekMUSE...)			E	M	R
d. MOOs (multiuser object oriented room) (LambdaMOO...)				E	M/R
e. MUSHs (multiuser shared hallucination)				E	M/R
f. Avatars				E	M/R
g. Video teleconferencing				E	M/R
6. Considering Accessing People's Original Information (Primary Sources) Through the Internet					
a. Personal websites (autobiographies, diaries, speeches, eyewitness accounts, letters, interviews, columns, commentaries, photos, results of original research...)		E	E	M	R
b. Statistics (census data, bureaucratic records...)		E	E	E	M/R

E = Emerging, M = Mastering, R = Reinforcing, P = Primary (gr. K–2), I = Intermediate (gr. 3–5), M = Middle School (gr. 6–9), H = High School (gr. 10–12), + = Postsecondary

7. Considering Accessing People's Interpreted Information (Secondary, Tertiary Sources) Through the Internet	P	I	M	H	+
a. Reference sites (atlases, dictionaries, encyclopedias, manuals, handbooks, almanacs. . .)		E	E	M	R
b. Periodical sites (newspapers, magazines, yearbooks, journals. . .)		E	E	M	R
c. Virtual museums and archives (toymuseum.com, watt.emf.net/, dreamscape.com/frankvad/tours.html. . .)		E	E	M	R
d. Virtual libraries (www.gutenberg.org,, vlib.org . . .)		E	E	M	R
e. Government sources (census, bureaucratic records. . .)		E	E	E/M	R
f. Graphics (clip art, graphics, photos. . .)		E	E	M	R
g. 3D graphics (Cult 3D, Live Picture Viewer. . .)		E	E	M	R
h. Animation clips (Flash Player. . .)		E	E	M	R
i. Video clips (from the Internet, video camera, VCR, TV. . .)		E	E	M	R
j. Audio clips (MP3 music, speeches, tape recordings. . .)		E	E	M	R
k. Radio (RealPlayer, Media Player, QuickTime. . .)		E	E	M	R
l. Television (RealPlayer, Media Player, QuickTime. . .)		E	E	M	R
8. Considering Traditional Sources					
a. Paper-based sources (encyclopedias, reference books, nonfiction, fiction, biography, technical books. . .)					
b. Other (microfiche, film, slides, recordings. . .)					
9. Considering Contemplative Thinking					
a. Drawing on your own thought processes to access creative thinking on the topic (original thought, opinion, intuition, theory . . .)					

ACCESSING

E = Emerging, M = Mastering, R = Reinforcing, P = Primary (gr. K–2), I = Intermediate (gr. 3–5), M = Middle School (gr. 6–9), H = High School (gr. 10–12), + = Postsecondary

2D. *Accessing* Technology Skill Sets	P	I	M	H	+
1. Considering Other Software for Accessing Data					
a. Word processor to record data (Word, Works, AppleWorks, WordPerfect...)		E	E	E/M	R
b. Database program to organize data (Access, Approach, Filemaker Pro...)		E	E	E/M	R
c. Spreadsheet program to arrange data (Excel, Works, QuattroPro...)		E	E	E/M	R
d. Graphics programs for using a scanner to digitally scan in photos, graphics (Photoshop, PhotoDeluxe, PhotoImpact...)		E	E	E/M	R
e. Graphics programs to digitally modify photos, graphics (Photoshop, PhotoDeluxe, PhotoImpact...)		E	E	E/M	R
f. Optical character recognition (OCR) program to scan text (OmniPage, Textbridge Pro...)		E	E	E/M	R
g. Voice recognition software to record speech (NaturallySpeaking, ViaVoice, VoiceXpress...)			E	E/M	R
2. Considering Possible Hardware for Accessing Data					
a. Internet service provider (ISP) for accessing the Internet (MSN, AOL...)		E	E	M	R
b. Basic computer (keyboard, mouse, monitor...) for accessing the Internet and storing data	E	E	E	M	R
c. Inexpensive Internet personal access devices (e.g., WebTV)	E	E	M	M	R
d. Back-up storage device (hard drive, Zip drive, read/write CD drive...) for safe storage of software and recorded data		E	E	M	R
e. CD ROM for accessing prerecorded data or music	E	E	M	R	
f. Multimedia computer for viewing and recording video		E	E	M	R
g. Local area network for accessing local computer data and software	E	E	M	R	
h. Modem for accessing the Internet		E	M	M/R	
i. Scanner for recording photos and graphics		E	M	M/R	
j. VCR for viewing video tapes and recording TV programs and video tapes	E	E	M	R	
k. Photographic camera (film, digital) for recording photographs	E	E	E/M	R	
l. Tape recorder for recording and playing interviews and sounds	E	M/R			
m. Video camera (VHS, digital) for recording interviews and other live action	E	E	M	M/R	

E = Emerging, M = Mastering, R = Reinforcing, P = Primary (gr. K–2), I = Intermediate (gr. 3–5), M = Middle School (gr. 6–9), H = High School (gr. 10–12), + = Postsecondary

2E. *Accessing* Review Skill Sets	P	I	M	H	+
1. Student Process Review Skill Set					
a. Reviews process by comparing progress to date with initial goals	E	M	R		
b. Considers relevance of accessed resources in relation to the original topic			E	M	R
c. Reviews the match between the data gathered, the teacher's purpose, and the student's purpose			E	M	R
d. Determines whether sources are properly documented (bibliography, footnotes, credits, attributions, quotes...)			E	M	R
e. Revisits original instructions to determine if scope of task was fully explored		E	M	R	
2. Collaborative Process Review Skill Set					
a. Works with others (peers, teacher, family) to review process by comparing progress to date with initial goals	E	M	R		
b. Works with others to revisit original topic and develops follow-up questions			E	M	R
c. Works with others in using existing data to further clarify boundaries of topic			E	M	R
d. Works with others to revisit original instructions to determine if scope of task was fully explored		E	M	R	
e. Uses self-assessment and collaborative Skill Set to determine if topic is practical		E	E	M	R
3. Teacher Process Review					
a. Review of teacher's *Accessing* goals and results					

ACCESSING

Stage 3: *Analyzing*

Skills for Analyzing Data from the Internet and Other Sources

Analyzing is the organizing and assembling stage of the NetSavvy process. As the data are checked for relevance to the topic, accuracy, and authenticity, it begins the process of data being turned into usable information. Students determine if the assembled data are sufficient to answer the questions or whether more research is necessary. Documentation of data is a vital part of the *Analyzing* stage.

E = Emerging, M = Mastering, R = Reinforcing, P = Primary (gr. K–2), I = Intermediate (gr. 3–5), M = Middle School (gr. 6–9), H = High School (gr. 10–12), + = Postsecondary

3A. *Analyzing* Essential Skill Sets	P	I	M	H	+
1. General Analyzing Skill Set					
a. Selects materials appropriate for reading and listening level of assignment			E	E	M
b. Recognizes suitability of data for own level of understanding		E	E	E/M	R
c. Identifies intended audience of data		E	E	M	R
d. Identifies whether sufficient detail has been provided			E	E	M
e. Considers different perspectives provided by different data sources				E	M
f. Considers sources that provide alternate points of view		E	E	M	R
g. Recognizes digressions from the main idea of a subject			E	E	M
h. Selects key sentences to use in note taking and quotations		E	E	M	R
i. Shares data with others to establish whether the information need has been met		E	E	E/M	R

A
N
A
L
Y
Z
I
N
G

E = Emerging, M = Mastering, R = Reinforcing, P = Primary (gr. K–2), I = Intermediate (gr. 3–5), M = Middle School (gr. 6–9), H = High School (gr. 10–12), + = Postsecondary

2. **Critical Analyzing Skill Set**	P	I	M	H	+
a. Recognizes digressions from the main idea of a subject			E	E	M
b. Distinguishes between fact and fiction (misconceptions, lies, deceit...)	E	E	E	M/R	
c. Distinguishes between fact and opinion		E	E	M/R	
d. Distinguishes between objective and subjective opinion			E	E	M/R
e. Distinguishes between fact and theory				E	M
f. Distinguishes between hypothesis and evidence			E	E	M
g. Distinguishes between hypothesis and generalization			E	M	R
h. Identifies unstated assumptions			E	E	M/R
i. Recognizes stereotyping			E	E	M/R
j. Identifies ambiguous arguments or claims			E	M	R
k. Recognizes the effect of placing contrasting text and images side-by-side		E	E	M	R
l. Interprets symbolism or metaphors contained in data			E	E	M/R
3. **Media Analyzing Skill Set**					
a. Identifies different media products (commercials, journals, political publications, informercials, advertising, promotional materials...)		E	E	E/M	R
b. Analyzes underlying meaning in commercial public media (newspapers, magazines, TV, radio, the Internet...)			E	E/M	R
c. Understands purpose of media products (selling products, influencing opinion, informing the public...)		E	E	E/M	R
d. Analyzes visual elements of media products (color, composition, graphical design, symbolism...)		E	E	E/M	R
e. Analyzes sound elements (mood, emotion, tone...)		E	E	E/M	R
f. Analyzes print elements (font, bolding, italics, color, style...)		E	E	E/M	R
g. Interprets how aspects of a media product combine to communicate		E	E	E/M	R
h. Analyzes how message is influenced by the media format used		E	E	E/M	R
i. Identifies best format for the topic (print, slide, film, sound...)		E	E	E/M	R

ANALYZING

E = Emerging, M = Mastering, R = Reinforcing, P = Primary (gr. K–2), I = Intermediate (gr. 3–5), M = Middle School (gr. 6–9), H = High School (gr. 10–12), + = Postsecondary

4. General Documenting Skill Set	P	I	M	H	+
a. Determines proper documentation (bibliography, credits, quotations...)			E	M	R
b. Checks dates data were created, published, or revised and considers their value in light of their age			E	M	R
c. Determines if the conclusions are justified by the data presented			E	E	M
d. Identifies ambiguous claims or arguments			E	E	M
e. Identifies digressions from the main idea of the subject			E	E	M
f. Determines if author presents original material (or compiles other sources)			E	M	R
g. Decides the significance of a text to own experiences and values			E	E/M	R
5. Documenting Skill Set—Internet (See Figures 7.2 & 7.3)					
a. Checks dates data were created, posted, or revised and considers their value in light of their age	E	E	M	R	
b. Checks that a qualified writer takes responsibility for the material and is accessible (e-mail address, personal web page, or through an Internet search engine) if there is a need to query the data	E	E	E/M	R	
c. Checks a person's signature file (e-mail, newsgroup, mailing list) to consider their qualifications in relation to the topic at hand	E	E	E/M	R	
d. Checks writer's intent in a newsgroup or mail list by using the carbon copy feature to determine the writer's intended audience	E	E	E/M	R	
e. Evaluates currency, credibility, suitability, and usability of on-line data	E	E	E	M/R	
f. Is skeptical about face value of multimedia data (since the appearance of a publication is not necessarily relevant to the quality of its data)	E	E	E/M	R	
g. Checks links in web site for comprehensiveness (links to Gopher, FTP sites...)	E	E	E/M	R	

ANALYZING

E = Emerging, M = Mastering, R = Reinforcing, P = Primary (gr. K–2), I = Intermediate (gr. 3–5), M = Middle School (gr. 6–9), H = High School (gr. 10–12), + = Postsecondary

6. Critical Authenticating Skill Set	P	I	M	H	+
a. Determines if data are skewed or manipulated through sources, viewpoint, or time			E	E	M/R
b. Determines if experts in the field agree on the findings			E	E	M
c. Understands how geographical source of data may limit their application				E	M/R
d. Identifies hidden or underlying messages			E	E	M
e. Recognizes propaganda, politics, lies, half-truths, hype, myths, and bandwagons			E	E	M
f. Identifies hidden agendas			E	E	M
g. Identifies digressions from the main idea of the subject			E	E	M
h. Determines if the work updates or substantiates knowledge on the subject			E	M	R
i. Determines a writer's values, assumptions, and biases			E	M	R
j. Considers evidence by taking into account who made, the observation, how it was made, and under what conditions			E	M	R
k. Assesses the logical validity of an argument (an author's personal experience is generally not considered sufficient evidence)			E	E/M	R
l. Determines if conclusion of a deductive argument is implicit within its premises			E	E/M	R
m. Determines that the premises of an inductive argument are true and the conclusion logically follows			E	E/M	R

A
N
A
L
Y
Z
I
N
G

E = Emerging, M = Mastering, R = Reinforcing, P = Primary (gr. K–2), I = Intermediate (gr. 3–5), M = Middle School (gr. 6–9), H = High School (gr. 10–12), + = Postsecondary

3B. *Analyzing* Prerequisite Skill Sets	P	I	M	H	+
1. General Thinking Skill Set					
a. Listens, observes, and reads with a purpose	E	E	E/M	M	R
b. Identifies main ideas and supporting details	E	E	E/M	M	R
c. Reads to find answers to specific questions	E	E	M	R	
d. Sifts to recover good data and reject bad data		E	E	E/M	R
e. Learns by sharing ideas with others	E	E	M	R	
f. Is aware of one's own political, cultural, and moral values			E	E	M/R
2. Critical Thinking Skill Set					
a. Questions the clarity of the data		E	E	M	R
b. Questions the accuracy of the data		E	E	M	R
c. Questions the precision of the data		E	E	M	R
d. Questions the relevance of the data		E	E	M	R
e. Questions the superficiality of the data			E	E	M/R
f. Questions the breadth of the data			E	E	M/R
g. Questions the logic of the data			E	E	M/R
3C. *Analyzing* Techniques Skill Sets					
1. Considering Methods for Analyzing Data					
a. Diagrams for graphically representing data		E	E	M	R
b. Webs for showing the connections between data		E	E	M	R
c. Categories for organizing and arranging data	E	E	E	M	R
d. Outlines for summarizing data		E	E	M	R
e. Paraphrasing for restating data		E	M	R	
f. Sequencing for ordering data	E	E	M	R	
g. Note cards for sorting data	E	E	E	M	R
h. Databases for organizing and recording data		E	E	M	R
i. Spreadsheets for arranging and recording data		E	E	M	R

ANALYZING

E = Emerging, M = Mastering, R = Reinforcing, P = Primary (gr. K–2), I = Intermediate (gr. 3–5), M = Middle School (gr. 6–9), H = High School (gr. 10–12), + = Postsecondary

3D. *Analyzing* Technology Skill Sets	P	I	M	H	+
1. Considering Computer Software for Analyzing Data					
a. Diagramming programs (Inspiration, Illustrator, Freehand, AppleWorks...)		E	E	M	R
b. Idea and concept mapping (Inspiration, CMap, LifeMap, Model-It...)		E	E	M	R
c. Outlining programs (Inspiration, AppleWorks, MSWord...)		E	E	M	R
d. Charting programs (Excel, AppleWorks...)		E	E	M	R
e. Note-carding programs (Hyperstudio, QuickCard...)		E	E	M	R
f. Database programs (Access, FileMaker Pro, R:base...)		E	E	M	R
g. Spreadsheet programs (Excel, Lotus 1-2-3, AppleWorks, QuattroPro...)		E	E	M	R
2. Considering Computer Hardware for Analyzing Data					
a. Uses computer for word processing, mapping, database...		E	E	E	M/R
3E. *Analyzing* Review Skill Sets					
1. Student Process Review Skill Set					
a. Reviews process by comparing progress to date with initial goals	E	M	R		
b. Reviews the match between the data gathered, the teacher's purpose, and the student's purpose			E	M	R
c. Revisits original instructions to determine if scope of task was fully explored		E	M	R	
2. Collaborative Process Skill Set					
a. Works with others (peers, teacher, family) to review process by comparing progress to date with initial goals	E	M	R		
b. Works with others in using existing data to further clarify boundaries of topic			E	M	R
c. Works with others to revisit original instructions to determine if scope of task was fully explored		E	M	R	
d. Uses self-assessment and collaborative Skill Set to determine if topic is practical		E	E	M	R
3. Teacher Process Review					
a. Review of teacher's *Analyzing* goals and results					

A N A L Y Z I N G

Stage 4: *Applying*

Skills for Applying Information from the Internet and Other Sources to Create Presentations and Products

After the material has been organized and analyzed, it must be presented in a finished form or product. For brevity in this Skills Framework, we apply the term "presentation" to all student outcomes. During the *Applying* stage, presentations are created in a variety of ways using combinations of the four flavors of information—text, images, video, and sound. As the presentation is developed, the process of turning data into information and usable knowledge is completed.

E = Emerging, M = Mastering, R = Reinforcing, P = Primary (gr. K–2), I = Intermediate (gr. 3–5), M = Middle School (gr. 6–9), H = High School (gr. 10–12), + = Postsecondary

4A. *Applying* Essential Skill Sets	P	I	M	H	+
1. Skill Set for Preparation of Material from Several Sources					
a. Creates a word bank (directional words, instructional words, action words, naming words...)		E	E	M	R
b. Creates an outline (list, mind map, visual web, storyboard...) to describe the sequential stages of the presentation		E	E	E	M/R
c. Edits for errors, omissions, and lack of clarity		E	E	M	R
d. Checks the instructional sequence for the desired result and makes the necessary modifications		E	E	M	R
e. Utilizes peer editing techniques to ensure the instructional sequence produces the desired result		E	E	M	R
2. General Presentation Skill Set					
a. Summarizes the main ideas		E	M	R	
b. Identifies relationships and patterns		E	E	M	R
c. Sorts information into categories		E	E	M	R
d. Arranges information in sequence		E	E	M	R
e. Arranges information within categories		E	E	M	R
f. Arranges categories in a logical order		E	E	M	R
g. Makes connections and draws inferences		E	E	M	R
h. Examines and integrates alternative points of view		E	E	E	M/R
i. Makes generalizations		E	E	E	M/R
j. Concludes with a summary		E	E	M	R

APPLYING

E = Emerging, M = Mastering, R = Reinforcing, P = Primary (gr. K–2), I = Intermediate (gr. 3–5), M = Middle School (gr. 6–9),
H = High School (gr. 10–12), + = Postsecondary

	P	I	M	H	+
3. Graphics Presentation Skill Set					
a. Organizes material according to presentation need (sequentially, randomly, in groups, linking pieces...)		E	E	E	M/R
b. Labels material (titles, comments, credits...)	E	E	E	M	R
c. Chooses style, materials, colors, textures		E	E	E	M/R
d. Recognizes the effect of color and style on mood and content		E	E	E	M/R
4. Writing Presentation Skill Set					
a. Converts the outlined steps of the planning stage into concise, grammatically correct sentences		E	E	M	R
b. Creates illustrations and captions for clarification of the text (diagrams, maps, charts, graphs...)		E	E	M	R
c. Forms sentences into paragraphs that have main ideas and detail sentences		E	E	M	R
d. Writes clear transitions between ideas, sentences, paragraphs, and drawings		E	E	M	R
e. Determines the reading level of the intended audience and edits accordingly for readability		E	E	E	M/R
f. Proofreads the text for grammatical structure, capitalization, spelling, and punctuation		E	E	M	R
g. Proofreads to ensure illustrations and captions correlate with the text		E	E	M	R

APPLYING

E = Emerging, M = Mastering, R = Reinforcing, P = Primary (gr. K–2), I = Intermediate (gr. 3–5), M = Middle School (gr. 6–9), H = High School (gr. 10–12), + = Postsecondary

5. Technical Writing Presentation Skill Set	P	I	M	H	+
a. Determines the reading level of the intended audience and writes accordingly for readability		E	E	E	R
b. Converts the outlined steps of the planning stage into concise, grammatically correct technical instructions		E	E	M	R
c. Creates technical illustrations and captions for clarification of the text (diagrams, maps, charts, graphs...)		E	E	M	R
d. Forms sentences into paragraphs that have main ideas and detailed instructions using technical words		E	E	M	R
e. Uses directional words (left, right, up, down, in, out...)		E	E	M	R
f. Uses instructional words (locate, find, summarize...)		E	E	M	R
g. Uses action words (turn, open, close, push...)		E	E	M	R
h. Uses naming words (wire, cable, button, disk...)		E	E	M	R
i. Shows the interrelationships—the integrated system formed by the parts		E	E	E	M/R
j. Writes clear transitions between ideas, sentences, paragraphs, and drawings		E	E	M	R
k. Proofreads the text for technical accuracy, grammatical structure, capitalization, spelling, and punctuation		E	E	M	R
l. Proofreads to ensure illustrations and captions correlate with the text		E	E	M	R
m. Proofreads to ensure that technical illustrations correlate with written instructions		E	E	M	R
6. Oral Presentation Skill Set					
a. Checks the acoustics or need for a microphone		E	E	M	R
b. Considers using illustrations, props, or gestures		E	E	M	R
c. Speaks using appropriate voice, pitch, and volume		E	E	M	R
d. Speaks with proper enunciation			E	M	R	
e. Speaks without word substitutions or repetition		E	E	M	R
f. Speaks with phrasing and expression that reflects punctuation			E	M	R	
7. Debating Skill Set					
a. Presents constructive speech, rebuttal speech, and cross-examination,		E	E	E	M/R
b. Makes complete source citations of evidence (author's name and qualifications, publication title, complete date, and page number)		E	E	M	R
c. Challenges fabrication and distortion		E	E	E	M/R
d. Understands and obeys the set rules of debating		E	E	E	M/R

APPLYING

E = Emerging, M = Mastering, R = Reinforcing, P = Primary (gr. K–2), I = Intermediate (gr. 3–5), M = Middle School (gr. 6–9), H = High School (gr. 10–12), + = Postsecondary

	P	I	M	H	+
8. Audio Presentation Skill Set					
a. Understands basic principles of audio production needed to create effective presentations (dubbing, editing, special effects, music, narration…)		E	E	E	M/R
b. Understands the point of view of the audience and ensures a comfortable physical environment for listening		E	E	M	R
9. Video Presentation Skill Set					
a. Understands basic principles of video production needed to create effective presentations (storyboarding, framing, zooming, panning, narration, music…)		E	E	E	M/R
b. Understands the point of view of the audience and ensures a comfortable physical and viewing environment		E	E	M	R
10. Multimedia Presentation Skill Set					
a. Understands basic principles of media production needed to create effective presentations (composition, design, editing, color, music…)		E	E	E	M/R
b. Understands the point of view of the audience and ensures a comfortable physical and visual environment for viewing		E	E	M	R
11. Internet Publishing Presentation Skill Set					
a. Netiquette Skill Set for appropriate use of the Internet		E	E	M	R
b. E-mail Skill Set for preparing postings to listservs and newsgroups		E	E	M	R
c. Multimedia presentation Skill Set for creating presentations for web sites (personal home page, educational site…)		E	E	M	R
12. General—Finalizing the Preparation of a Presentation					
a. Reviews to delete repetitive and irrelevant information.		E	E	M	R
b. Reviews to determine if there is too much or not enough information		E	E	E	M/R
c. Checks vocabulary, sentence structure, and mechanics		E	E	M	R
d. Checks if the findings support or refute the original ideas contained in the topic		E	E	E	M/R
e. Reexamines information for relevance to intended focus and format		E	E	E	M/R
f. Finds new examples, explains events and actions to further emphasize the point		E	E	E	M/R
g. Considers new conclusions based on accumulated information		E	E	E	M/R
h. Finalizes the bibliography and footnotes		E	E	M	R
i. Does final edit or rehearsal of presentation		E	M	R	

APPLYING

E = Emerging, M = Mastering, R = Reinforcing, P = Primary (gr. K–2), I = Intermediate (gr. 3–5), M = Middle School (gr. 6–9), H = High School (gr. 10–12), + = Postsecondary

4B. *Applying* Prerequisite Skill Sets (See Figure 8.2)	P	I	M	H	+
1. Basic Skill Set for Preparation of a Presentation					
a. Can identify basic needs (materials, equipment, space, time, and personnel)		E	E	M	R
b. Can identify needed outside help and determine how to get it		E	E	M	R
c. Can identify other resources needed		E	E	M	R
d. Can identify the best learning style in which a task can be presented (visual, auditory, tactile, written work) and convert it into other learning styles if necessary			E	E	M/R
e. Can define potential problems in completing an assignment and indicate where opportunities exist for alternate solutions		E	E	M	R
2. General Presentation Skill Set Using Graphics					
a. Can present materials in graphic form (drawings, graphs, photos, art…)		E	E	M	R
b. Can operate necessary equipment for creating graphics for use in a presentation		E	M	R	
3. General Presentation Skill Set Using Writing					
a. Can address barriers to effective writing (materials, writing environment, personal physical problems, learning disabilities…)			E	M	R
b. Can determine format details (type of paper, cover, fonts, style…)		E	M	R	
c. Can restate, summarize, and paraphrase information		E	E	M	R
d. Can locate answers to questions from resources		E	E	M	R
e. Can verify information		E	E	M	R
f. Can consider including other knowledgeable opinions		E	E	M	R
g. Can document information (bibliography, footnotes, credits, and quotations)		E	E	M	R
4. General Technical Writing Presentation Skill Set					
a. Can differentiate between and use technical and nontechnical writing formats		E	E	M	R
b. Can compare and contrast the language used in technical and nontechnical writing		E	E	M	R
c. Can compare and contrast the objective of technical and nontechnical writing		E	E	M	R
5. General Audio Presentation Skill Set					
a. Can operate tape player effectively (record, dub, edit, play…)	E	E	M	M/R	
6. General Video Presentation Skill Set					
a. Can operate VCR and monitor effectively (record, dub, edit, play…)	E	E	M	M/R	

A P P L Y I N G

E = Emerging, M = Mastering, R = Reinforcing, P = Primary (gr. K–2), I = Intermediate (gr. 3–5), M = Middle School (gr. 6–9), H = High School (gr. 10–12), + = Postsecondary

7. General Multimedia Presentation Skill Set	P	I	M	H	+
a. Can use word processing program	E	E	E	M	R
b. Can use graphics software to enhance presentations		E	E	M	M/R
c. Can prepare charts, graphs, or tables		E	E	M	M/R
d. Can incorporate computer-generated graphics into presentation		E	E	M	M/R
e. Can incorporate audio into presentation		E	E	M	M/R
f. Can incorporate video into presentation		E	E	M	M/R
8. General—Consults with a Teacher or Peers for:					
a. Edits (reviewing information to delete repetitive and irrelevant information)		E	E	M	M/R
b. Proofs (checks for vocabulary, sentence structure, and mechanics)		E	E	M	M/R
c. Checks for flow (coherence and mechanics)		E	E	M	M/R
d. Rehearsing the presentation		E	E	M	M/R
e. Ensuring extra effort is made to do a good job		E	E	M	M/R
4C. *Applying* Techniques Skill Sets (See Figure 8.2)					
1. General Considerations					
a. Considers barriers to an effective presentation		E	E	E	M/R
b. Considers presentation formats in relation to topic (graphical, written, audio, video, multimedia. . .)		E	E	E	M/R
c. Considers presentation formats in relation to the Skill Set of the presenter		E	E	E	M/R
d. Considers presentation formats in relation to the needs of the intended audience		E	E	E	M/R
2. Graphics					
a. Considers graphical components to be used as part of presentation (map, graph, picture, model, illustration, cartoon, time line. . .)		E	E	E	M/R
b. Considers a completely graphical presentation (slide show, art show, computer graphics. . .)		E	E	E	M/R
3. Writing					
a. Formal writing (report, essay, article. . .)		E	E	E	M/R
b. Personal writing (journal entry, short story, letter, poem. . .)	E	E	E	E	M/R

A P P L Y I N G

E = Emerging, M = Mastering, R = Reinforcing, P = Primary (gr. K–2), I = Intermediate (gr. 3–5), M = Middle School (gr. 6–9),
H = High School (gr. 10–12), + = Postsecondary

	P	I	M	H	+
4. Technical Writing					
a. Technical report (science project, psychological or sociological study…)		E	E	E	M/R
b. Computer programming (set of programming instructions, small program)		E	E	E	M/R
c. Instructional guide (set of technical instructions, documentation, manual…)		E	E	E	M/R
5. Oral Presentation					
a. Written speech		E	E	M	R
b. Speech from notes		E	E	M	R
c. Speech without notes		E	E	E	M/R
d. Interview (with student, family, community member…)		E	E	E	M/R
e. Dramatic presentation (play, re-enactment, role playing…)		E	E	M	R
f. Literary presentation (poetry reading, literary selection…)		E	E	M	R
6. Debate					
a. One-on-one		E	E	M	R
b. Group		E	E	M	R
7. Audio Presentation					
a. Voice recording (interview, speech, report, story…)	E	E	E	M	R
b. Musical recording (singing, musical instrument…)	E	E	M	R	
8. Video Presentation					
a. Video recording (interview, speech, report, story, musical presentation…)	E	E	E	M	R
b. Animation (cartoon, claymation, digital…)	E	E	E	M	R
9. Multimedia Presentation					
a. Computer presentation (live, interactive, viewer driven…)		E	E	M	R
b. Combinations of audio, video, and graphics (tape recorder, video camera, VCR, still photography, graphical images…)		E	E	M	R
10. Internet Publishing					
a. Web site (personal home page, educational site, commercial site…)		E	E	E	M/R
b. E-mail (person-to-person, listserv, and newsgroup postings…)		E	E	M	R

E = Emerging, M = Mastering, R = Reinforcing, P = Primary (gr. K–2), I = Intermediate (gr. 3–5), M = Middle School (gr. 6–9), H = High School (gr. 10–12), + = Postsecondary

4D. *Applying* Technology Skill Sets (See Figure 8.2)	P	I	M	H	+
1. Using Hardware					
a. Multimedia computer		E	E	E	M/R
b. VCR	E	E	M	M/R	
c. Video editing equipment		E	E	M	M/R
d. Tape player	E	E	M	M/R	
e. Audio editing equipment		E	E	E	M/R
f. Photocopier	E	E	E	M/R	
2. Using Computer Software					
a. Drawing and graphing programs (CorelDRAW, Illustrator, Freehand, Excel...)		E	E	M	R
b. Word processing programs (Word, WordPerfect...)		E	E	E	M/R
c. Databases to present information (Lotus Notes, FileMaker, AppleWorks...)		E	E	E	M/R
d. Sound editing software (Premiere, Avid Cinema, Director...)		E	E	E	M/R
e. Video editing software (Premiere, Avid Cinema, Director...)		E	E	E	M/R
f. Multimedia presentation programs (Premiere, PowerPoint, Hyperstudio, Kai's Power Show, MovieWorks, Avid Cinema, Director...)		E	E	E	M/R
g. Publishing programs (PageMaker, Quark XPress...)		E	E	E	M/R
h. Internet publishing programs (PageMill, Acrobat, HomePage...)		E	E	E	M/R
4E. *Applying* Reviewing Skill Sets					
1. Student Self-Assessment Questionnaire					
a. How did you feel after completing your presentation?		E	M	R	
b. How did your intended audience respond? (teacher, peers, family...)		E	M	R	
c. What advice did people offer?		E	M	R	

APPLYING

E = Emerging, M = Mastering, R = Reinforcing, P = Primary (gr. K–2), I = Intermediate (gr. 3–5), M = Middle School (gr. 6–9), H = High School (gr. 10–12), + = Postsecondary

2. Collaborative Process Review Skill Set	P	I	M	H	+
a. Works with others (peers, teacher, family) to review process by comparing progress to date with initial goals	E	M	R		
b. Works with others to revisit original topic and develops follow-up questions			E	M	R
c. Works with others in using existing data to further clarify boundaries of topic			E	M	R
d. Works with others to revisit original instructions to determine if scope of task was fully explored			E	M	R
e. Uses self-assessment and collaborative Skill Set to determine if topic is practical		E	E	M	R
3. Teacher Process Review					
a. Review of teacher's *Applying* goals and results					

**A
P
P
L
Y
I
N
G**

Stage 5: *Assessing*

Skills for Assessing the Presentation and the Process

Assessing is the final stage of the NetSavvy process. It operates at two levels. One level focuses on assessing the presentation that has been developed by the student. The other assesses the process that the teacher and student have undergone in completing the project. Assessment of both the presentation and process by the student, the teacher, and others is critical to the learning experience. Assessment confirms that learning has occurred, while allowing students to make connections to previous experiences, as well as laying the groundwork for dealing with future information problems.

E = Emerging, M = Mastering, R = Reinforcing, P = Primary (gr. K–2), I = Intermediate (gr. 3–5), M = Middle School (gr. 6–9), H = High School (gr. 10–12), + = Postsecondary

5A. *Assessing* Essential Skills (See Figure 9.2)	P	I	M	H	+
1. Presentation Self-Assessment Questionnaire					
a. What were my goals?		E	E	E	M/R
b. Were my goals achieved?		E	E	E	M/R
c. What knowledge have I gained?		E	E	E	M/R
d. What Skill Set have I acquired?		E	E	E	M/R
e. What did others think of my work?		E	E	E	M/R
f. What impact did my work have?		E	E	E	M/R
g. How well does this project stand alone?		E	E	E	M/R
h. Which elements were well developed?		E	E	E	M/R
i. Which were partially developed?		E	E	E	M/R
j. Which weren't developed at all?		E	E	E	M/R
k. What should be done differently in the future?		E	E	E	M/R
l. What should be done better in the future?		E	E	E	M/R
m. What was the most difficult and why?		E	E	E	M/R
n. What was enjoyed the most and why?		E	E	E	M/R
o. What was enjoyed the least and why?		E	E	E	M/R

A
S
S
E
S
S
I
N
G

E = Emerging, M = Mastering, R = Reinforcing, P = Primary (gr. K–2), I = Intermediate (gr. 3–5), M = Middle School (gr. 6–9), H = High School (gr. 10–12), + = Postsecondary

	P	I	M	H	+
2. Technique Assessment Questionnaire					
a. What were the strong and weak parts of the *Asking* methods and tools?					M/R
b. What were the strong and weak parts of the *Accessing* methods and tools?					M/R
c. What indexing systems were most useful for *Accessing* data?		E	E	E	M/R
d. What were the strong and weak parts of the *Analyzing* methods and tools?					M/R
e. What were the strong and weak parts of the *Applying* methods and tools?					M/R
f. What were the strong and weak parts of the *Assessing* methods and tools?					M/R
3. Technology Assessment Questionnaire					
a. What equipment, hardware, and software were best for accessing data?		E	E	E	M/R
b. What equipment, hardware, and software were best for analyzing data?		E	E	E	M/R
c. What equipment, hardware, and software were the best for applying the information?		E	E	E	M/R
4. Process Assessment Questionnaire					
a. How could the initial instructions (*Asking*) have been improved?		E	E	E	M/R
b. How could the researching (*Accessing*) of the data have been improved?		E	E	E	M/R
c. How could the processing (*Analyzing*) of the data have been improved?		E	E	E	M/R
d. How could the presentation (*Applying*) of the information have been improved?		E	E	E	M/R
e. How could your assessment (*Assessing*) of the data have been improved?		E	E	E	M/R
5. Transfer of Learning					
a. To academic subjects (science, social studies, math)		E	E	E	M/R
b. To nonacademic subjects (music, sports, playing a game, working in a business)		E	E	E	M/R
c. To personal life (career, hobby…)		E	E	E	M/R
d. Comparing outcome with other schools, districts, states, countries		E	E	E	M/R
5B. *Assessing* Prerequisite Skill Sets					
1. Starting Point Skill Set					
a. Appreciates the value of an outside point of view (the observations of others)		E	E	M	R
b. Appreciates the value of reflection and self-examination		E	E	M	R
c. Understands the nature of the learning process		E	E	E	M/R
d. Appreciates the value of the process as well as the outcome		E	E	E	M/R

A
S
S
E
S
S
I
N
G

E = Emerging, M = Mastering, R = Reinforcing, P = Primary (gr. K–2), I = Intermediate (gr. 3–5), M = Middle School (gr. 6–9), H = High School (gr. 10–12), + = Postsecondary

5C. *Assessing* Technique Skill Sets (See Figure 9.2)	P	I	M	H	+
1. Considering Presentation Assessing Methods					
a. Teacher assessment (test, marks, verbal, checklist, notes...)		E	E	M	R
b. Student self-assessment (reflection, notes, checklist, questionnaire...)		E	E	M	R
c. Peer assessment (verbal, checklist, questionnaire...)		E	E	M	R
d. Collaborator assessment (verbal, checklist, questionnaire...)		E	E	M	R
e. Live audience assessment (verbal, notes...)		E	E	M	R
f. Internet audience assessment (e-mail, number of hits, number of links...)		E	E	M	R
g. Student, parent, or teacher assessment of the possible transfer of learning (to other work, to other school subjects, to self, to the future...)		E	E	M	R
2. Considering Process Assessing Methods					
a. Teacher assessment of student process (test, marks, notes, verbal...)		E	E	M	R
b. Student assessment of student process (reflection, notes...)		E	E	M	R
c. Teacher assessment of teacher process (reflection, notes...)		E	E	M	R
d. Student assessment of teacher process (verbal, notes...)		E	E	M	R
e. Others' assessment of teacher's and student's processes (verbal, notes...)		E	E	M	R
f. Assessment of the assessing tools used (verbal, checklist, questionnaire...)		E	E	M	R
g. Assessment of the possible transfer of learning (to other work, to other school subjects, to self, to the future...)		E	E	E	M/R

ASSESSING

E = Emerging, M = Mastering, R = Reinforcing, P = Primary (gr. K–2), I = Intermediate (gr. 3–5), M = Middle School (gr. 6–9), H = High School (gr. 10–12), + = Postsecondary

5D. *Assessing* Technology Skill Sets (See Figure 9.2)	P	I	M	H	+
1. Presentation Assessing Tools					
a. Written assessment of student (test, letter grade, percentage, teacher checklist, teacher notes, live audience questionnaire, Internet audience response…)		E	E	M	R
b. Verbal assessment of student (questions, comments, or voting by teacher, collaborators, peers, audience…)		E	E	M	R
c. Contemplative assessment (student self-assessment)		E	E	M	R
2. Process Assessing Tools					
a. Written assessment (checklist, notes…)		E	E	M	R
b. Verbal assessment (questions, comments by teacher, collaborators, peers…)		E	E	M	R
c. Contemplative assessment (student self-assessment)		E	E	M	R
5E. *Assessing* Reviewing Skill Sets					
1. Teacher Review of *Assessing*					
a. Teacher review of student *Assessing* work					
b. Teacher review of *Assessing* goals and results					
2. Project Review by Others					
a. Student review of the overall project					
b. Other's review of the overall project					

Part IV

Overcoming Educational Obstacles and Assumptions

How do we set the stage for successful implementation of NetSavvy skills across the curriculum in all disciplines? How do we avoid falling into the trap of yet another educational "initiative du jour" that quickly ends up discarded and forgotten? How do we integrate the 5As of InfoSavvy as they apply to the Internet, otherwise known as NetSavvy skills, into our instructional strategies? How can we ensure with confidence that our efforts will improve the information-processing and thinking skills of all students?

Detailed and practical answers to each of these important questions were provided in Part II, Chapters 4 through 9, in the form of a series of student and teacher NetSavvy Tools that are designed and aligned to work with the Skills Framework.

Staging for the successful integration of NetSavvy skills requires systematic intervention in the learning experiences of students starting as early as kindergarten. However, we need to consider a number of obstacles that once understood can be overcome from the outset. We have identified five main categories of obstacles facing educators today, which we present as five separate chapters in this section. These categories are as follows.

- Chapter 10 discusses "Assumptions About the Agenda" and explains why and how we teach what we teach.

- Chapter 11 discusses "Assumptions About Learning" and focuses on our initial assumptions about what we believe our students already know.

- Chapter 12 covers "Assumptions About Information" and addresses the differences between traditional paper-based information and electronic information.

- Chapter 13 deals with "Assumptions About Technology in Education" and identifies our understanding about what instructional technology can do.

- Chapter 14 discusses "Assumptions About Assessment" and considers how we evaluate student learning (which in turn determines academic success) and how typically what is going to be tested is usually what gets learned.

Each chapter is structured so that we present the bad news first and hold the good news for last. The good news is that once these obstacles are fully understood, they can be transformed into tremendous opportunities to facilitate the successful implementation of NetSavvy information processing and thinking skills into all instructional strategies and all learning environments. Let's consider each of these obstacles in detail in the next five chapters.

Chapter 10

Obstacle 1: Assumptions About the Agenda

Why Do Teachers Do What They Do?

Some teachers believe in project-based, cooperative learning environments, whereas others prefer traditional didactic lecture methods. Some are willing to experiment with the new information technologies to see how they can be effective in student learning, whereas others feel that it's a waste of time to move away from tried and tested practices. What are the agendas that drive an educator's activities and behaviors? We believe that there are two types of agendas that determine instructional strategies and actions: intrinsic agendas and extrinsic agendas.

The intrinsic agendas are based on a teacher's personal experiences, interests, special expertise, and deeply held values. National, state, district, and school prescriptions, as well as the job market and postsecondary educational requirements, dictate the extrinsic agendas. Some agendas may be very explicit, such as a state curriculum, while others are mostly implicit, such as when the culture of a school imposes itself on a teacher's thinking, possibly without the teacher being consciously aware of it.

These agendas originate from just about everywhere—from the state, community, workplace, economy, politics, culture, tradition, social structures, school administration, school district, curriculum, teachers, parents, and students. In this respect, education is unlike any other business. Although many businesses focus on a main product or service, education deals with providing a range of services for children in partnerships with virtually every aspect of society. At least, that's the theory.

In reality the state curriculum dominates all the other agendas. Since the state curriculum is supposed to represent the amalgamation of all these agendas, some may question if there is anything wrong with this. The problem lies in the fact that bureaucracies detached from most of the stakeholders usually manage state agendas. There is no formal process in place for the ongoing incorporation of all these agendas, particularly the student agenda. Consequently, the curriculum can easily become irrelevant to the learners for whom it was designed. Students live, breathe, and play in the real world that exists outside of education, and they bring an immediacy of that world into their classrooms. The more archaic and disconnected the curriculum becomes, the more disengaged students become from what and how they learn.

Let's check out this statement by taking a short test. Have you ever heard any of your students, or your own children ask one or more of these questions? How about all of them?

- Why should I learn this?
- What does it mean?
- When will this be over?
- Why do I need to know this?
- Will I ever use this?
- When will I ever use this?
- Does this count?
- Will this be on the test?

These are some of the indicators that instruction is happening in a vacuum, especially when such questions are asked repeatedly. They reveal that personal connections between the students and the curriculum are not being made. If this is happening, real learning is probably not taking place. Students can learn content out of context for an exam, and some students are particularly good at it. In many cases, these are the students who are proclaimed to be academically successful. However, a few weeks later, it's likely that much of this learned content will be lost or forgotten by these same students.

At this point, it's important to ask the question "What exactly is curriculum?" The Industrial Age mindset asserts that the curriculum is the business of school. It can be determined at the national, state, and district levels and is frequently imposed upon teachers by a traditional, hierarchical system of management. In reality, the word "curriculum" is often used as a vague and confusing piece of jargon, understood by only a few, mainly those who wrote it.

As a result, there is a great deal of focus on the learning of content that has been fragmented into a number of subject areas prescribed by the curriculum guide. Traditionally, this content is delivered in a series of Carnegie instructional units that are each approximately 45 minutes in duration. Despite the fact that a majority of students are capable of mastering the material if enough time is provided, the amount a student learns is typically the variable while the allotted time for learning is the constant. The degree of mastery of content is measured by exams at the end of a prescribed number of weeks. Scores on these exams largely determine the academic success needed to graduate from most educational institutions. The traditional agenda disregards a huge body of evidence about how learning occurs. It tends to discount the idea that different learners may have different learning rates and learn in different ways. With time as the constant and learning as the variable, our current agenda is no longer viable, particularly given what we know about learning in the Information Age.

Are we suggesting the abandonment of the traditional curriculum or that content isn't important? Absolutely not! However, we are suggesting that this is the perfect time to reconsider and work to transform the long-standing agenda of schools.

Transforming the Agenda

We have a wonderful opportunity to reconnect the curriculum to parts of the world often considered to be on the outside of education. These include the community, the workplace, and the home. In doing so, we have the chance to recontextualize learning and make it more relevant to the needs of our children. To do this, educators must understand the great opportunity that awaits them at this crossroads, where a new direction offers a way to better serve the purpose of schools, education, teaching, and learning.

We can do this if we shift our focus away from the discipline by discipline memorization of content to the learning of content across disciplines. This occurs naturally in the process of developing the skills associated with problem solving, critical thinking, and information processing.

That is where this book can help. *NetSavvy* provides an organizer of many information literacy skills in the form of the Skills Framework as well as teacher and student tools aligned with and designed to work with the Skills Framework that together demonstrate how simply this can be accomplished. *NetSavvy* can lead you through the first steps of an exciting journey to create a new curriculum approach that more directly serves the current and future needs of all. Using the backdrop of the Internet as a major educational resource, we invite you to come along with us on a journey that can lead to a new way of teaching and learning.

Chapter 11

Obstacle 2: Assumptions About Learning

The Assumed Learnings

Young children entering school for the first time are carefully assessed, and a great deal of effort is put into making sure that a set of essential survival skills are learned. Most parents and early childhood educators know they cannot afford to make assumptions about their children's abilities and skills without putting them at great risk. However, as children move through the education system, larger and larger assumptions are made about what they already know and what they are capable of doing.

These assumed learnings are, in large part, the result of pressures the curriculum agenda places on teachers who normally have to cope with a wide range of readiness among the children who enter their classrooms. In the rush to cover the curriculum, educators may incorrectly assume their students have adequate information literacy skills, such as the ability to read, listen carefully, take notes, rephrase questions, describe what they have seen, or make a point coherently. This can result in serious gaps in some students' knowledge.

Many of these learning gaps, which went unnoticed in Industrial Age jobs, are increasingly being revealed in the emerging Information Age workplace. Current research indicates that one of every three adults in the United States is marginally or functionally illiterate. Yet with the proliferation of e-mail and Internet-based information, the skills of reading and writing have become even more important than ever before.

If you are comfortable in your ability to address the individual needs of your students, you are ready to integrate NetSavvy or InfoSavvy skills into your instructional practices. If you feel that you have made certain assumptions about your students' information-processing skills in the past and have then been disappointed when your expectations haven't been met, Part II will be especially helpful for you.

Transforming Our Assumptions About Learning

How do we begin to turn the issue of assumptions into a great opportunity? The detailed Lesson Planners in Part II are structured to take into account our assumptions about student learning. We believe that most assumptions are made about the foundational competencies that promote reading, writing, speaking, and listening skills. These are the building blocks or "givens" for all students and the prerequisite skills for information fluency. Once these skills are in place, they form a solid foundation for developing the more complex skills of the 5As of NetSavvy.

By examining our assumptions and checking the skill level of students, we ensure that the prerequisite skills are either already in place or can be introduced and practiced during any learning activity. This advance knowledge of individual student learning deficiencies leverages a teacher's ability to customize or tailor specific portions of any learning activity to that student. This is a powerful way of establishing a solid foundation for developing the art and craft of information literacy for every student. It makes irrelevant a student's age, speed of learning, learning style, or grade level.

Chapter 12

Obstacle 3: Assumptions About Information

The Changing Nature of Information

In the good old days of paper, pen, and ink, there seemed to be some permanence and stability attached to information. The business of publishing involved professional editors and a lengthy process including editing, revising, peer reviewing, proofing, and checking for veracity, authority, and authenticity. This formalized method resulted in the shaping and predigestion of information deemed fit for public consumption. Educational institutions created an extra step: a rigorous adoption system, which could require several years, before a textbook was allowed into a school. These editing formalities were performed by a variety of professionals. The result was considered to be authoritative information, although in the adoption process many primary sources were filtered and refined into secondary and tertiary products. Although secondary sources can be of great value, a significant amount of important information from primary sources would be filtered out. But to be published, an author needed to have credentials or connections of some sort. Having a good idea or great manuscript wasn't enough. In an instant, the Internet has changed all of this.

Today we face a new and dramatically different world. In something called cyberspace, the rules about how information can be published have been reinvented. Traditional publishing remains an important source of information. In fact, primarily as a result of the information explosion, the industry now publishes more materials than ever. However, the Internet has thrown the old notion of what is fit for public consumption right out of the window. Today, basically anything goes! How can this be? It's the direct result of many outstanding and relatively unappreciated features of the Internet, which may be summarized as follows:

- Grants every user unprecedented power to do three important things: to research, to communicate, and to publish

- Replaces many costly activities, but is relatively inexpensive to use

- Can be totally personal, as in e-mail, or very public, as in on-line journals, chat rooms, newsgroups, or Internet conferencing

- Provides anytime, anywhere, global access to information

- Provides cutting edge information, often as an event happens
- Is relatively democratic and neutral: age, sex, culture, color, and bias are all irrelevant when a user can self-publish at will
- Is unregulated so that it can become a propaganda tool—any interest group or organization can write whatever they want, whenever they want
- Bypasses all print-publication formalities, doing away with the gateway function of the traditional publishing establishment
- Has the capacity for hyperlinking every bit of information to every other bit of information in an easily accessible network that is limitless in size
- Allows almost instantaneous indexing and accessing of every word, unlike the limited indexes in books

This is quite a list! For some, the lush world of cyberspace is eagerly welcomed as an escape from the flat, two-dimensional aspects of paper-based resources. On the other hand, some educators and decision makers regard the Internet as a wolf in sheep's clothing. They consider it to be a wasteland of unedited information, disguised in alluring colors, shapes, sizes, and flavors and dressed up in an exciting medium that draws in people, particularly the young and naive, and dazzles them.

There is no doubt that the Internet is an absolutely unparalleled tool for researching current factual information. With a minimum of effort, anyone can put a single word in an Internet search engine and in seconds receive a torrent of information. More importantly, a NetSavvy user of an Internet search engine can put in a little more effort and receive one perfect hit, or a dozen good ones, instead of the same hits buried in millions of other totally irrelevant hits. This is in stunning contrast with the prospect of trying to find a single word in just one paper-based book, especially when the word may not be listed in the index, if there is an index.

Some schools, not wanting to be left out, have rushed out to get wired and jacked in, only to be faced with the challenge of trying to figure out how to filter out the questionable information accessed by students. This can be done by using software to deny access to certain types of sites, but more than 50% of students already have access to the Internet at home. As a result, an increasing number of students can already access the good, the bad, and the ugly information right from their homes regardless of school filtering policies. Never before have we experienced so much free access to virtually any type of information, both in and out of school. But ask any "Net" generation student how they feel about their access being restricted by filtering software, and many will matter-of-factly tell you to do whatever you want, because they'll figure out how to get around it anyway. Most of them are a lot smarter than we give them credit for. Whether we like it or not, many of our children are already deeply connected.

Are you frustrated? Are you ready to throw up your hands in submission? Are you thinking that there is no way that we can change the obstacles into opportunities? Not only *can* we change things; it's imperative that teachers *do* take advantage of the Internet as an educational resource.

Transforming Our Assumptions About Information

Okay you say, where's the opportunity and what's the reason for pursuing it? The opportunity lies in the very nature of the Internet itself. Youngsters find this a very cool place to hang out and chat with friends from all over the world. It's their electronic playground. We can take advantage of this. Because good information is nestled in between misinformation, disinformation, and even unsuitable information, it's the perfect medium for our students to learn, practice, and master the skills of information literacy. Unlike any other resource, the Internet not only brings all of this to our very fingertips, but it also easily connects us with people around the globe. Most things that exist in the real world also exist in cyberspace. The Internet is simply a mirror of the real world, representing the very best, as well as the very worst, of humanity. There are, however, several big differences. The differences lie in the fact that in the cyberworld, time and distance are compressed, and there are no geographical obstacles, travel limitations, or border checkpoints. And, unlike the real world, the cyberworld can be disconnected at the flick of a switch.

We've given some reasons why teachers should use the Internet but let's just say it like it is. The main reason why students need to experience the full potential of the Internet is much more than that it's a cool tool or that it's entertaining, or even that it's a great medium for teaching information literacy skills. It's really simple. The Internet is growing exponentially and has evolved overnight into a full-fledged, commercial medium. More than 90% of our students who are in schools today will graduate into a world where the cybermarketplace will be seamlessly integrated with the real world marketplace.

Our students will have to work, play, live, and learn with this twin world. It's our job as educators to help them prepare for this new reality. To do this, they have to be NetSavvy so they can function in the networked world of digital information and virtual people, while at the same time they need to be InfoSavvy to function in the world of paper-based information and real people. These are exciting times! Never before in our history have we had to prepare our students to live in two worlds simultaneously. Yes, it really is that simple and that's probably why it may be so difficult for some people to accept.

Beyond these compelling reasons, let's consider the opportunities. Being connected is much more than just having access to the Internet, e-mail, and digital data. It's about having access to the world and being able to communicate with it in real time. To do this, we must create real world relevance and context for all our learning activities. We can bring experts, scientists, writers, speakers, politicians, and poets right into our classrooms. Or, we can go out and arrange to meet them at their place of work. We can visit virtual museums, zoos, and art galleries around the world and take field trips to what David Thornburg describes as "any number of geographically scattered sacred sites of learning" without ever having to fill out another field trip form ever again.

The Internet also provides us with an opportunity to observe and practice the rules and code of human conduct. We know that just as we have rules or etiquette for behavior in the real world, similar rules or "Netiquette" can and must be established for working in cyberspace. Morals, good manners, and working and playing safely are as important on the Internet as they are in the real world. The choice of whether to filter digital information is a professional decision made by decision makers to fit into their value systems and routines. Whether we filter and slow release digital information from the Net or let our students have unrestricted access, it's the perfect opportunity to help them learn and develop their own intellectual filters for flourishing in the digital world as well as in the physical world. They know that it's important to learn and work with traditional and digital information responsibly and that proper etiquette and Netiquette are essential for success. They look to teachers to guide them through this complex dual world.

Chapter 13

Obstacle 4: Assumptions About Technology in Education

The Technological Challenge

By taking an historical perspective of technology in considering its relationship with education over the course of the last few centuries, we can understand why there is serious confusion among educators about the role technology should play in education. During this time, education has moved from being no-tech to low-tech and now to high-tech. Some suggest that other than the overhead projector, blackboard, duplicating machine, and the school intercom, most technologies have had little impact on instruction. It is suggested that the reason certain technologies did take root was because they served to maintain the status quo of Industrial Age structures, supporting and propagating the centralized authority and one-way flow of information. Consequently, despite major changes in the rest of society, schools have shown a remarkable resistance to significant change, let alone technological change.

In earlier times, education was done verbally in a no-tech environment. Low-tech blackboards, chalk, and slates didn't appear until the early 1830s. Even pencils, erasers, pens with ink, pencil cases, or mass-produced textbooks only became common during the early part of the 20th century. Medium-tech technologies such as radios, duplicating machines, overhead projectors, filmstrips, and TVs appeared between the 1920s and 1960s. All of these were considered to be high-tech products at the time, and each technology advance was heralded as the one that would revolutionize education. Such promises were never fully realized, and each time, after a brief honeymoon, education pretty much returned to business as it had always been.

Little did we realize that a number of separate technological innovations would come together in the late 1970s, giving birth to an amazing new technology, the personal computer. When combined with the sudden emergence of the Internet, these two precocious children have quickly developed into unruly adolescents who strongly resist regulation. As a result, they are presently busy challenging the establishment in every way they can as they grow into full adulthood. In concert with other emergent information technologies, they are irrevocably reshaping our educational and social landscapes. This time, there is no escape for schools.

The tens of billions of dollars spent on educational technology in the United States over the last 5 years bears testament to education's commitment to the reform and improvement of schools. However, as we examine the results, we realize that educators have made the assumption that they can address the emergence of technology into our lives simply by adding a new subject in the school curriculum—technology. The thrust of this new subject is the learning of the mechanics of hardware and software. This is like suggesting that the appropriate use of pencils or televisions should be taught by studying the mechanics of pencils and televisions. How did this happen? Further examination reveals an assumption that learning about technology is a natural process that happens osmotically simply by placing the technology in close proximity to the users. As a result of this assumption, most of the available dollars have been spent on acquiring hardware and software, leaving far too little money to thoroughly train educators about how technology can be used to support and enhance learning.

Very little effort has been made to help educators learn to use technology to do new things in different ways With the exception of a few pockets of exemplary innovative use of the new technologies, most teachers remain in the dark. Other than the isolated teaching of Hyperstudio, Netscape, Internet Explorer, PowerPoint, or Microsoft Word, many teachers have reverted to doing what they have always done, only now they do it with flashy new high-tech tools.

As an example, consider the common practice of getting students to write a composition with pen or pencil. Only after it has been manually written are students allowed to take it to the lab so that a "good copy" can be done at the computer. While many may consider this to be an acceptable practice, using a computer merely as a typewriter is a sad underutilization of the capacity of the technology. Such "just-in-case" learning of isolated skills outside of a real context will most certainly fail to engage most students in effective learning. Using a computer for writing is not just about teaching them how to keyboard or how to use a word processor, or even how to become a stenographer—the goal should be to teach students how to communicate effectively, responsibly, and thoughtfully. Learning about the keyboard or how to use the word processor is merely an incidental but essential by-product of this process.

Today's writing must go well beyond the basic skills. The writing process should be a great opportunity to use drawings, clip art, or photos; to incorporate the principles of page layout and design; to understand the power of color, fonts, and white space; or even to be an opportunity to do research and publish the results on the Internet.

Teachers have been placed at tremendous risk by the sin of "assumicide"—the act of the "assumed learnings" discussed earlier. They have huge missing links in conceptualizing how the new high-tech tools can be used to promote higher-level thinking skills or to create strategic learning environments. To continue doing what they have always done and to resist new ways of approaching learning means that many teachers can no longer do their jobs effectively. As a result, many long-standing educational practices are coming under scrutiny or becoming increasingly marginalized.

Before we look at the opportunities offered by educational technology, let's consider some questions. Is technology just a tool? Yes and no! While technology can be easily seen as providing new tools that allow us to do new things or to do old things better, it also directly shapes our thinking and practices in vast, unseen ways. For instance, who would have thought that the invention of the wheel would lead to wagons, to automobiles, to trains, and even to planes? Understanding that those who live by the crystal ball usually end up eating crushed glass, who is willing to project what the Internet will do to teaching and learning?

Thus, in working with the tools in Part II, it will pay to be cautious as you consider the possibilities of what technology can or cannot do. Our thinking is limited by our perceptions. How we think can hold us back, preventing us from seeing things from a different point of view. As we move forward, we ask that you reconsider your traditional assumptions about teaching and learning. What will it take to transform these assumptions about educational technology so that we can begin to create meaningful learning environments that no student will be able to resist?

Transforming Our Assumptions About Technology in Education

Let's put the issues of educational technology to one side for a moment. Why did you become an educator? It certainly wasn't a get-rich scheme was it? You had a mission and that mission gave you focus. Your intention was to make a difference in the lives of children. Do you remember? For anyone reading this, we know your focus is to help students learn the skills and behaviors that will allow them to stand on their own and function effectively once they leave your care. It's the view of the authors that being successful at this has far less to do with teaching chemistry, math, or social studies than it has to do with developing the essential skills for information literacy that are needed to cope successfully. That is the focus of this book.

How can we make things so attractive that no kid can refuse to come to our classes? We aren't talking about entertainment or infotainment here. We're talking about turning kids on to learning. Consider this scenario: I'm a high school teacher. My students need to create and understand graphs, learn how to extrapolate and predict trends, and show how graphs can create false impressions. How do I go about teaching this? What context can I use that will help them to make connections to the real world and real life? Is there software or hardware that can help me teach this concept? Should I go low-tech or high-tech? What tools would work best for me, given the fact that more than 80 percent of students are visual and kinesthetic learners? Should they work in pairs, in groups, or as individuals? Who can help me determine the best course of action?

All of these questions have more to do with creating context and relevance to learning experiences than they do to the use of specific hardware or software. The technology skills that are learned by students and teachers during these activities will simply be an incidental, but important, by-product of the particular exercise. Using graphing software or a graphic calculator could work as well in a math or science class as it would in this example of a PE class where the teacher has to "cover" aerobic fitness and nutrition from the curriculum guide by having students examine their own cardiovascular health and eating habits. It's only when learning becomes personalized that it becomes relevant and interesting!

In the end, it really doesn't matter what the subject area is because the tools work well almost anywhere *if* teachers are willing to exercise their imaginations in developing innovative, thought-provoking ways to help students learn a certain aspect of the curriculum. Technology should not be an issue until it can do something that will facilitate learning. Technology is not used just for the sake of using it. The total focus is on the students and learning, not the tools. In the end it's not so much a matter of rethinking our assumptions about technology, but about rethinking our attitudes about teaching.

Chapter 14

Obstacle 5: Assumptions About Assessment

What Constitutes Academic Success?

The assumptions made about how students are evaluated underpin the four issues previously outlined. As a result, the way that assessment is done has a significant influence on how the agenda, learning, information, and technology are delivered.

Traditionally, student learning has been measured by testing intended to demonstrate an understanding of factual content. This worked well in a time when factual content was the cornerstone of a system based on the needs of the Industrial Age workplace. In today's Information Age, a system of assessment based on content no longer completely reflects the needs of the workplace or society. It's part of our responsibility to make sure that it does. Although content is still important, much more is expected of the Information Age worker. But the assumption remains that we *know* how well students are doing based primarily on their letter grades or test scores. Many teachers will readily acknowledge that traditional tests access only limited aspects of what students may have learned and almost never measure how students use what they know. In reality, what is going to be on the test is given more time as it's covered by teachers. Over time, the limited subset of content covered by this test model tends to become the major focus of the de facto curriculum.

The marks issued by schools, colleges, and universities are ingrained in the psyche of parents, employers, and society as the sum total of what a student knows. A letter grade or percentage is viewed as an abbreviated statement of a student's core competencies in a subject. These units of evaluation lead to "credits," which are only assigned if the student completes the required number of seat hours followed by "successful" test results. These become the assumptions that underscore the rites of passage to graduation at all levels of education. Sadly, the biggest assumption is that we *really* understand what a score, grade, or a credit means. Educator and writer Bill Spady describes this assumption by asking, What does an 86 for your child's achievement represent? Just accept it, he asserts, as millions of other American parents do. He reminds us that these were the scores that got us through the Cold War in one piece and that the colleges need them because otherwise they wouldn't know who is smart enough to understand the professors. Spady explains that with a 70 your child can get into a community college and with an 80 into a four-year college. So you can assume that 86 is very good, and only four points away from being gifted. But a 95, he states, will get your child into the door of just about any place—except the Information Age....

Consider for a moment a student's high school transcript.

- What does a student's grade mean?
- What portion of a student's learning and achievement does a test represent?
- What does a grade "prove" about the student, the school, or the district?
- What does a grade indicate about the school or district that needs to be improved?
- What does a grade indicate about students' learning that their teachers don't already know?
- What does a particular grade fail to measure that is essential to students' success in the Information Age? Why don't we measure and report that as well?

Moving Beyond Letter Grades and Test Scores

Due to the rapid proliferation of information technologies across the globe, we are being drawn deep into an Information Age, where it's essential to reconsider what it means to be intelligent, educated, and academically successful. Many of the new skills needed in today's workplace are process skills, such as the ability to think independently, to work in teams, to be flexible, to be critical thinkers, to manage time and information, and to develop healthy levels of emotional intelligence. One current problem is that there is nothing to stop a teacher from testing students' knowledge of a process by giving them a test that merely measures their level of factual knowledge of the process. There is a factual component to the learning, but testing only for facts is a poor measure of the total learning that takes place. When only factual content is tested for, it will receive the focus of teaching and learning. The important process skills that result in deeper learning will be omitted or treated as unimportant. Even if the process skills are mastered, such learning will go unacknowledged and unrewarded.

It's clear that this new set of skills will inevitably become an essential part of the mainstream curriculum because it forms the basis of what it means to be literate in the Information Age. But these skills cannot easily be measured using our traditional means of assessment. For the development of these important skills in students to be acknowledged, our means of assessment must change.

Some K–12 educators may agree with many of the statements above. But such statements can also quickly raise their ire, because they feel powerless to change a system seen as being driven by the traditional requirements and expectations set forth by colleges, universities, parents, and business—expectations that continue to be based on an Industrial Age mindset for schools. As we continue to debate why we should change or how we should change, we are rapidly reaching the point where change will probably overrun our institutions before we decide to invite it in. Meanwhile, the personal interview that forms a key step in the normal hiring process in the new workplace continues to reflect, in part, the failure of the current grading system to adequately convey to an employer the practical skills that a prospective employee may have. These skills, such as being a good team player, critical thinker, or problem solver, are the ones that are becoming more and more necessary in the workplace.

The reluctance of the school system to alter its traditional method of assessment is one of the main reasons why spending billions on technology has failed to deliver the anticipated impact on student learning. Consider the difference between learning the facts about driving a car by reading a driver training manual and learning the process of how to drive a car by getting behind the steering wheel. The core skill—the process of maneuvering a large machine between the white lines—is not something that would be properly measured by a test of the factual knowledge contained in the manual. Of course, this is why there is an actual driving test as well as a written test. It's the process-oriented driving test that measures the students' success at critical thinking and problem solving—making sudden judgment calls in real-life situations in traffic. It's also a measure of their success at how to think independently while working in a team—driving the car while dynamically interacting with pedestrians and other drivers. Thus in the real world of driver testing, it's normal to test process skills as well as factual knowledge.

Can you imagine if you only had to pass a written test to get a driver's license? To be fair, schools do provide limited experience in processes, perhaps the equivalent of some driving experience in your own driveway. But it's when a student takes on a real-life task that deep learning occurs. The type of learning that comes with driving at full speed in rush hour or operating a clutch in traffic up a steep hill on a rainy night.

Likewise, to learn the technology of a major word processing program, it's not enough to read a 1,000-page manual while studying the different features under each menu and trying a few examples. True learning occurs when the word processor is used as a tool in the process of doing a meaningful task.

Many teachers understand that today's curriculum is largely disconnected from real life. This results in many students having substantial gaps in the foundational skills necessary for the Information Age. New technologies can play an important role in creating project-based, student-centered learning environments in which multiple intelligences and differences in learning styles can be honored. But as the focus of instruction changes from a primary emphasis on facts to an increased emphasis on process, the means of assessing success must be modified to parallel those changes.

Transforming Our Assumptions About Assessment

To transform the assumptions about assessment into an opportunity is to accept the challenge of renegotiating our teaching and learning contract with our students. Students look to us for guidance and support. The new contract is very simple and it looks like this: Teachers continue to present what skills and knowledge students should have, while more student-orientated project-based learning provides greater recognition of their individual wants, needs, and learning styles. We believe that being InfoSavvy and, in particular, becoming NetSavvy, must be a large part of this new contract.

Are we suggesting individualized learning programs for our students? Eventually yes, but just as our children must learn new skills, we must first build strong foundations for creating new learning and teaching environments. Some of these environments are focused in the classroom, whereas others are focused in the digital world. Just like our children, we must first learn how to sit up and crawl before we learn to walk. This takes time, appropriate training, and a long-term commitment to restructuring our educational system from kindergarten well into postsecondary education. Every journey starts with a few steps in the right direction, and that is where this book can really help.

This book is devoted to helping you use the Internet to get moving in the right direction. To this end, we have created the following NetSavvy aids:

- A NetSavvy Skills Framework that outlines a set of skills necessary to develop information literacy as it pertains to using the Internet
- A series of NetSavvy tools that assist students in processing digital information
- A series of NetSavvy tools that can help teachers to integrate NetSavvy skills into any content area of the curriculum

The evaluation tools emerge directly out of the Skills Framework, which addresses the traditionally measurable aspects of learning, as well as those areas that are not usually measured. Using the principles of constructivism, learning styles, collaborative teamwork, individualization, and project-based learning, the examples demonstrate what is possible. Ultimately, this is limited only by our educational imagination—all of which has little to do with levels or priorities of funding, district or state policies, the need to cover the curriculum guide, getting ready for the test, or any of the other issues that have traditionally driven education. The journey is ours to take. Together with our students, we can learn to navigate the vast oceans of information found on the Internet. This approach lends itself perfectly to teaching, learning, practicing, and assessing information literacy skills. We are here to help you to optimize the conditions for learning and to offer guidelines for the steps to be taken.

What Could This Look Like?

Consider the following scenario: A group of five senior students are working collaboratively in a virtual classroom. Each student is affiliated with a different school from a different part of the globe. They have been developing a working relationship over the Internet with the help of their teachers and new communications technologies. Having negotiated a 2-week period for completing their project, they are busy creating a Web-based product that will demonstrate their understanding of tornadoes. Whereas half of their grade is based on the content that is produced, the other half is based on an evaluation of the processes they use to create the product. The main processes assessed are the collaboration of the students with each other and the demonstration and application of the knowledge gained through a public presentation designed to help the public understand tornadoes. Each student brings a set of talents and strengths to the table, and each must take responsibility to help the group, their teachers, and the public gain a better understanding of the intricacies of tornadoes. The students evaluate themselves and their teachers at the same time their teachers evaluate them. As they assess the effectiveness of their information-processing skills (the 5As), their teachers watch, helping to facilitate the process.

How Do We Get There?

Being aware of the five obstacles that face all educators today has an empowering effect. Once they are confronted, understood, and dispelled, we can see that the obstacles are really opportunities on which to build a better learning environment and better schools. Decades ago, our system of assessment used content-based testing to do a good job of assessing student knowledge of the content-based curriculum. This served students well in preparing them for the Industrial Age world. Although we must continue to perform this function in the Information Age, there is even more to do. Our job demands that we work to keep our system of assessment relevant to an ever-changing world.

Chapter 15

The Case for NetSavvy

There can be no denying the vastness of the information landscape today. According to Neil Postman, in the United States alone there are more than 12,000 newspapers, 12,000 periodicals, 37,000 video outlets, 600 million radios, 300 million TVs, 200 million computers, and more than 500 million Web pages. There are 300,000 books published annually. Every day 165 million pieces of junk mail are sent and 41 million photographs are taken. Millions of sources of information all over the world come at us through every possible channel and medium including light waves, air waves, fiber, cable, computer banks, telephones, copper wires, satellites, and printing presses.

Yet it was only in the 1970s that the computer chip totally transformed the world of electronics. It was only in the 1980s that computers deeply penetrated the world of big business. And it has only been in the 1990s that we have ourselves witnessed the personal computer invading small businesses and reaching into the homes of most ordinary people. Very soon we will see the vast majority of businesses and consumers become wired together by the Internet and the resulting profound transformation of the retail and service industries.

You don't have to be a futurist to see that the way we do almost anything that uses information will soon be transformed as well, and it is getting easier to understand that education will be transformed in ways we can't even begin to imagine. It's time to make a bigger and better effort to help our students get ready to live in what has been silently solidifying around us—the Information Age.

Appendix A

Templates of the NetSavvy Teacher Tools

Ten-Minute Lesson Planner

1. ASKING (Framework, 1C Skill Sets)

Prerequisites (Framework, 1B Skill Sets)

2. ACCESSING (Framework, 2C Skill Sets)

Prerequisites (Framework, 2B Skill Sets)

Content

Prerequisite content knowledge

5. ASSESSING

Content to be assessed

Process skills to be assessed
(Framework, 5A Skill Sets)

Prerequisites
(Framework, 5B Skill Sets)

Connections

Curriculum

Outside school

3. ANALYZING (Framework, 3C Skill Sets)

Prerequisites (Framework, 3B Skill Sets)

4. APPLYING (Framework, 4C Skill Sets)

Consider what form student presentations will be in:

Paper-Based	Computer	Other
report	writing	oral
speech	drawing	audio
display	multimedia	video

Prerequisites (Framework, 4B Skill Sets)

Stage 1: ASKING Lesson Planner

1B. Asking Prerequisite Skills

Goal: to check your assumptions about what basic Asking skills students must already have

Basic Student Skills Needed
1. Observing   2. Listening   3. Speaking

Add any basic skills that are not included in the Skills Framework to the Essential Skills section below

1C. Asking Techniques Skills

Goal: to engage students in this topic by stimulating their interest to discuss the topic and ask questions

Possible Methods
Student Basic Asking Tool
Student Higher-Level Asking Tool

1. Brainstorming   2. Question Forming
3. General Conversing   4. Critical Conversing

1A. Asking Essential Skills

Goal: to identify the question-asking and conversing skills you want students to develop during the Asking stage of the project

1. Observing & Questioning   2. Listening & Questioning   3. Thinking & Questioning

Skills to be introduced

Skills to be reinforced

1D. Asking Equipment Needs

Goal: to ensure that the equipment needed to do the Asking stage is available and working properly

1. Software Needs
a. Word processor

b. Search engine

c. Idea and concept mapping

d. CD-Rom

e. Other

2. Hardware Needs
a. Computer

b. Other

1E. Asking Review Skills

Goal: to check that the Asking stage processes are properly and fully implemented

1. **Student Process Review**

2. **Collaborative Process Review**

3. **Teacher Process Review**

Stage 2: ACCESSING Lesson Planner

2B. Accessing **Prerequisite Skills**

Goal: to check your assumptions about what basic Accessing skills students must already have

Basic Student Skills Needed

1. General Workstation
2. General Computer
3. General Internet
4. Internet On-line
5. General Reading
6. Technical Reading

Add any basic skills that are not included in the Skills Framework to the Essential Skills section below

2C. Accessing **Techniques Skills**

Goal: to examine possible methods of Accessing data and choosing the best for this project

Possible Methods

Student Accessing Tool for Search Engines
Student Analyzing Tool for Web sites
Student Analyzing Tool for Documenting Sources
Accessing the Internet:

1. Starting Skills
2. Indexing Systems
3. Sources by Location
4. Communication
5. Sources—Real time
6. Primary Sources
7. Secondary Sources
8. Traditional Sources

2A. Accessing **Essential Skills**

Goal: to identify the skills you want students to develop during the Accessing stage of the project

1. Using Hardware
2. Using Software
3. Recording Data and Creating a Bibliography

Skills to be introduced

Skills to be reinforced

2D. Accessing **Equipment Needs**

Goal: to make sure that the equipment needed for Accessing sources is available and working properly

1. Software Needs
a. Word processor   b. Database   c. Spreadsheet
d. Scanner   e. Photos   f. OCR   g. Voice recognition

2. Hardware Needs
a. ISP b. Computer c. WebTV d. Backup storage
e. CD-ROM f. Multimedia g. LAN h. Modem i. Scanner
j. VCR k. Camera l. Tape recorder m. Video camera

2E. Accessing **Review Skills**

Goal: to check that the Accessing processes are properly and fully implemented

1. Student Process Review

2. Collaborative Process Review

3. Teacher Process Review

Stage 3: ANALYZING Lesson Planner

3B. Analyzing **Prerequisite Skills**

Goal: to check your assumptions about what basic Analyzing skills students should already have

Basic Student Skills Needed
1. General Thinking Skills

2. Critical Thinking Skills

Add any basic skills that are not included in the Skills Framework to the Essential Skills section below

3C. Analyzing **Techniques Skills**

Goal: to consider the best possible methods of Analyzing data

Possible Methods
Student Analyzing Tool for Web sites
Student Analyzing Tool for Documenting

a. Diagramming	b. Webs	c. Categorizing
d. Outlining	e. Paraphrasing	f. Sequencing
g. Note cards	h. Databases	i. Spreadsheets

3A. Analyzing **Essential Skills**

Goal: to identify the analyzing, documenting and authenticating skills you want students to develop during the Analyzing stage of the project

1. General Analyzing	2. Critical Analyzing	3. Media Analyzing
4. General Authenticating	5. Internet Documenting	6. Critical Authenticating

Skills to be introduced

Skills to be reinforced

3D. Analyzing **Equipment Needs**

Goal: to make sure that the equipment needed for Analyzing information is available and working

1. Software Needs
a. Diagramming software

b. Idea & concept mapping software

2. Hardware Needs

3. Other

3E. Analyzing **Review Skills**

Goal: to check that the Analyzing stage processes are properly and fully implemented

1. Student Process Review

2. Collaborative Process Review

3. Teacher Process Review

Stage 4: APPLYING Lesson Planner

4B. Applying Prerequisite Skills

Goal: to check your assumptions about what basic Applying skills students should already have

Basic Student Skills Needed for a Presentation

1. Preparation Skills   2. Graphics Skills   3. Writing Skills
4. Technical Writing   5. Audio Skills   6. Video Skills
7. Multimedia Skills   8. General

Add any basic skills that are not included in the Skills Framework to the Essential Skills section below

4C. Applying Techniques Skills

Goal: to consider the best possible methods for students to make (Apply) their presentations

Possible Methods
Student Applying Tool for Presentations

1. General   2. Graphic   3. Writing   4. Technical Writing
5. Oral   6. Debate   7. Audio   8. Video
9. Multimedia   10. Internet

4A. Applying Essential Skills

Goal: to identify the Applying skills you want students to develop during the preparation and presentation of their projects

1. Several Sources skills 2. General Presentation skills 3. Graphics skills 4. Writing skills
5. Technical Writing skills 6. Oral skills 7. Debating skills 8. Audio skills 9. Video skills
10. Multimedia skills 11. Internet skills 12. General

Presentation Skills to be introduced

Presentation Skills to be reinforced

4D. Applying Equipment Needs

Goal: to make sure that the equipment needed for Applying information is available and working properly

1. Hardware Needs
a. Multimedia computer b. VCR c. Video editing
d. Tape player e. Audio editing f. Photocopier

2. Software Needs
a. Drawing program b. Word processor c. Database
d. Sound editing program e. Video editing program
f. Multimedia program g. Publishing program
h. Internet publishing program

4E. Applying Review Skills

Goal: to assess that the Applying processes are properly and fully implemented

1. Student Process Review

2. Collaborative Process Review

3. Teacher Process Review

Jukes, I., Dosaj, A., & Macdonald, B. *NetSavvy: Building Information Literacy in the Classroom, 2nd Edition.* ©2000, Corwin Press, Inc.

Stage 5: ASSESSING Lesson Planner

5B. Assessing Prerequisite Skills

Goal: to check your assumptions about what basic Assessing skills students should already have

Basic Student Skills Needed for Being Assessed

Add any basic skills that are not included in the Skills Framework to the Essential Skills section below

5C. Assessing Techniques Skills

Goal: to consider the best possible methods of Assessing student processes and presentations

Possible Methods
1. Presentation Assessing Methods
Student Assessing Tool for Presentations
a. Teacher b. Student c. Peers d. Collaborators
e. Live audience f. Internet audience g. Other

2. Process Assessing Methods
Student Assessing Tool for Process Skills
a. Teacher b. Student c. Peers d. Collaborators
e. Live audience f. Internet audience g. Other

5A. Assessing Essential Skills

Goal: to identify the skills you want students to develop during the Assessing stage

1. Student Self-Assessing skills 2. Tool Assessing skills 3. Process Assessing skills
4. Technique Assessing skills 5. Technology Assessing skills
6. Transfer of Learning

Skills to be introduced

Skills to be reinforced

5D. Assessing Equipment Needs

Goal: to make sure that the equipment or material needed for Assessing is ready
1. Presentation Assessing Tools
a. Written (test, letter grade, percentage, checklist, notes, live audience questionnaire, Internet response...)
b. Verbal (questions, comments, voting by teachers, collaborators, peers, audience...)
c. Contemplative (student self-assessment)

2. Process Assessing Tools
a. Written (checklist, notes...)
b. Verbal (questions, comments by teachers, peers...)
c. Contemplative (student self-assessment)

5E. Assessing Review Skills

Goal: to check that the Assessing processes are fully and properly implemented
1. Teacher Review of Assessing
a. Teacher review of student assessing work
b. Teacher review of assessing goals and results

2. Project Review by Others
a. Student review of overall project
b. Others review of overall project

Appendix B

Templates of the NetSavvy Student Tools

Student Basic ASKING Tool

Project:_____Teacher:_____Student(s):_____

Topic:
Teacher's key words on this topic:

1. Background Questions—based on your own knowledge
What general knowledge do you have about this topic? From where?

Do you have any real world experiences or connections to this topic?

What are your key words about this topic?

2. Clarifying Questions—based on established knowledge
Use the key words on this page to form questions that will guide you in finding established information about the topic. Try starting your questions with words like How do...?, What do...?, When..?, Why...?, Where do...? and Who...?

Q1.	Q6.
Q2.	Q7.
Q3.	Q8.
Q4.	Q9.
Q5.	Q10.

Jukes, I., Dosaj, A., & Macdonald, B. *NetSavvy: Building Information Literacy in the Classroom, 2nd Edition.* ©2000, Corwin Press, Inc.

Student Higher-Level ASKING Tool

Project:_____Teacher:_____Student(s):_____

3. Current Questions—based on present-day thinking

Much of the information available today is based on established knowledge that has been accepted for a period of time. It may or may not be out of date with current thinking. Prepare questions on your topic in light of current trends by contrasting the past with the present and questioning or wondering about how the topic could be looked at differently.

Q1.

Q2.

Q3.

Q4.

Q5.

4. Futuristic Questions—based on imaginative thinking

Consider the established and current knowledge on your topic, together with your personal knowledge, and try to predict things about your topic that may be true in the future. Prepare the questions by imagining, forecasting, pretending, amplifying, inventing, estimating, contrasting, explaining, extrapolating, or applying a principle, for example— How will...?, What if...?, If this... then what...?

Q1.

Q2.

Q3.

Q4.

Q5.

Student ACCESSING Tool for Search Engines

Accessing topic: **Student(s):**

Search engine name (to be entered in Web browser location bar):

A. GENERAL SEARCH for_____

Make sure you use lower case and end your words with an asterisk (*) to avoid missing pluralized and other versions of your keywords.

Search language	Hits	Comment
1.	hits:	
2.	hits:	
3.	hits:	
4.	hits:	

B. SPECIFIC SEARCH for_____

Remember, for specific information, type in enough key words to narrow down the number of hits to the exact information you are looking for.

Search language	Hits	Comment
1.	hits:	
2.	hits:	
3.	hits:	
4.	hits:	

C. EXACT PHRASE SEARCH for_____

Now do an exact search using "quotation marks" around the key phrase of your question.

Search language	Hits	Comment
1.	hits:	
2.	hits:	
3.	hits:	
4.	hits:	

Student ANALYZING Tool for Web Sites

Student(s):_____Web site:_____http:_____

Content

	pick one	Explain your choice
1. Content excellent for your purpose	[5]	
2. Content good for your purpose	[4]	
3. Content helpful for your purpose	[3]	
4. Content poor for your purpose	[2]	
5. Content irrelevant for your purpose	[1]	

Organization Links

1. Web page of an organization/institute	[5]	
2. Web site linked to organization/institute	[4]	
3. A large independent Web site	[3]	
4. Small Web site with some simple links	[2]	
5. No relation to anything else	[1]	

Authorship

1. Author has reputation and credentials	[5]	
2. Author has interest and credentials	[4]	
3. Author has special interest in subject	[3]	
4. Author not very knowledgeable	[2]	
5. Author unknown	[1]	

Sources

1. Material is writers own research	[5]	
2. Material is based on primary sources	[4]	
3. Material closely linked to credible source	[3]	
4. Material seems based on secondary sources	[2]	
5. Sources unknown	[1]	

Authentication of Information

1. Author can be queried by e-mail	[5]	
2. Site can be reached by e-mail	[4]	
3. Site or author can be reached by mail	[3]	
4. Site or author can be reached by other means	[2]	
5. No way to reach author or the site	[1]	

Presentation

1. Web site is appealing or impressive	[5]	
2. Web site is perfectly fine for its purpose	[4]	
3. Focus is on presentation and not content	[3]	
4. Weak on content and presentation	[2]	
5. Very minimal effort on presentation	[1]	
Total Web site quality adds up to	___ /30	

Please add up your choices from each section. Circle the corresponding number and rating.

6 7 8 9 10	11 12 13 14 15	16 17 18 19 20	21 22 23 24 25	26 27 28 29 30
AWFUL	POOR	SATISFACTORY	GOOD	EXCELLENT

138

Student ANALYZING Tool for Documenting Sources

Project:_____ Teacher:_____ Student(s):_____

1. Web site:_____ http://_____

   Last modified: _____ Out of date?_____

   Subject:_____ Heading: _____

   Author: _____ Credentials: _____

   Employer: (self) (institution) (company) (society) (lobby) (group) (other):_____

   Perspective: (pro) (neutral) (con): _____

   Intended audience: (general) (schools) (adults) (special interest) (members) (consumers) (new members)
   (others):_____

2. Web site:_____ http://_____

   Last modified: _____ Out of date?_____

   Subject:_____ Heading: _____

   Author: _____ Credentials: _____

   Employer: (self) (institution) (company) (society) (lobby) (group) (other):_____

   Perspective: (pro) (neutral) (con): _____

   Intended audience: (general) (schools) (adults) (special interest) (members) (consumers) (new members)
   (others):_____

3. Web site:_____ http://_____

   Last modified: _____ Out of date?_____

   Subject:_____ Heading: _____

   Author: _____ Credentials: _____

   Employer: (self) (institution) (company) (society) (lobby) (group) (other):_____

   Perspective: (pro) (neutral) (con): _____

   Intended audience: (general) (schools) (adults) (special interest) (members) (consumers) (new members)
   (others):_____

Jukes, I., Dosaj, A., & Macdonald, B. *NetSavvy: Building Information Literacy in the Classroom, 2nd Edition.* ©2000, Corwin Press, Inc.

Student APPLYING Tool

Project:_____Teacher:_____Student(s):_____

Consider methods for creating a presentation

1. Graphics: map; graph; illustration...
2. Writing: report; essay; journal entry article; short story; letter; poem...
3. Technical writing: report; guide...
4. Oral: speech; interview; drama...
5. Debate: one-on-one; group...

6. Audio: interview; speech; story; musical recital ...
7. Video: video recording; animation...
8. Multimedia: audio; video; graphics; pictures; text
9. Internet publishing: Web site; personal e-mail; listserv posting; newsgroup posting...

Notes:

Consider tools for creating a presentation

1. Hardware
a. Multimedia computer
b. VCR
c. Video editing equipment
d. Tape player
e. Audio editing equipment
f. Photocopier
g. Other...

2. Software
a. Drawing/graphing program: _____
b. Word processing program: _____
c. Database program: _____
d. Sound editing program: _____
e. Video editing program: _____
f. Multimedia program: _____
g. Publishing program: _____
h. Internet publishing program: _____

Notes:

Checklist for creating a presentation

[ ] Have addressed the obstacles to creating an effective presentation

[ ] Have edited the work for spelling, punctuation & consistency

[ ] Have proofed the work for vocabulary & sentence structure

[ ] Have rehearsed & checked the work for flow

[ ] Have made extra effort to do an excellent job

[ ] To make my presentation better I can:

Jukes, I., Dosaj, A., & Macdonald, B. *NetSavvy: Building Information Literacy in the Classroom, 2nd Edition.* ©2000, Corwin Press, Inc.

Student ASSESSING Tool for Presentations

Project:_____Teacher: _____Student(s):_____

Assessing **Methods**—fill in with teacher at start of project

Considering Presentation Assessing Methods

a. Teacher assessment; b. Student self-assessment; c. Peer assessment; d. Collaborator assessment;
e. Live audience assessement; f. Internet audience assessment; g. Student, parent or teacher
   assessment of possible transfer of learning to job, to other school subjects, to self, to the future...

Notes:

Assessing **Tools**—fill in with teacher at start of project

Considering Presentation Assessing Tools

a. Written assessment tools: mark; test; letter grade; percentage; checklist; notes; live
   audience questionnaire; e-mail; Internet audience response...

Notes:

b. Verbal assessment tools: questions; comments; applause; voting...

Notes:

c. Contemplative self-assessment tools: questions; mark; notes; checklist; questionnaire—
   a sample is provided below...

Notes:

Presentation Self-Assessment Questionnaire—do just after presentation

What were my goals?

How were my goals achieved?

What new knowledge have I gained?

What new skills have I learned?

What impact has my work had on me?

What should be done differently in the future?

What was the most difficult & why?

What was least enjoyed & why?

What was most enjoyed & why?

Other comments:

Jukes, I., Dosaj, A., & Macdonald, B. *NetSavvy: Building Information Literacy in the Classroom, 2nd Edition.* ©2000, Corwin Press, Inc.

Student ASSESSING Tool for Process Skills

Project:_____Teacher:_____Student(s):_____

Instructions: Read each of the process skills and then circle the number 3, 2, 1 or 0 for that skill based on how you assess yourself in that particular skill. For example, if you understand the skill but need more practice, you would circle "2." The number of skills rated multiplied by 3 equals the maximum possible score.

Key
3 = I get it and feel I have a good handle on this skill
2 = I am getting it, but I really could do with some more practice
1 = I dont really get it and could do with some help
0 = This is a new topic. I don't understand what this is and need some help

Process skills	Before project	After project
1. Asking		
	0 1 2 3	0 1 2 3
	0 1 2 3	0 1 2 3
	0 1 2 3	0 1 2 3
	0 1 2 3	0 1 2 3
	0 1 2 3	0 1 2 3
2. Accessing		
	0 1 2 3	0 1 2 3
	0 1 2 3	0 1 2 3
	0 1 2 3	0 1 2 3
	0 1 2 3	0 1 2 3
	0 1 2 3	0 1 2 3
3. Analyzing		
	0 1 2 3	0 1 2 3
	0 1 2 3	0 1 2 3
	0 1 2 3	0 1 2 3
	0 1 2 3	0 1 2 3
	0 1 2 3	0 1 2 3
4. Applying		
	0 1 2 3	0 1 2 3
	0 1 2 3	0 1 2 3
	0 1 2 3	0 1 2 3
	0 1 2 3	0 1 2 3
	0 1 2 3	0 1 2 3
5. Assessing		
	0 1 2 3	0 1 2 3
	0 1 2 3	0 1 2 3
	0 1 2 3	0 1 2 3
	0 1 2 3	0 1 2 3
	0 1 2 3	0 1 2 3
	Total before	**Total after**

maximum possible score is number of skills X 3: _____ X 3 = _____.   _____ /_____   _____ /_____

Appendix C

Recommended Reading List

Beyond Technology: Questioning, Research and the Information Literate School by Jamie McKenzie, FNO Press, 2000, ISBN 0967407826

For more than 30 years, Jamie McKenzie, the editor of the highly respected *From Now On* web journal (www.fno.organization) has been working with teachers and media specialists to emphasize higher level thinking, problem solving and decision making. His newest book, *Beyond Technology: Questioning, Research and the Information Literate* brings the reader the best of the previously published articles about launching student research and resource-based learning.

Data Smog: Surviving the Information Glut by David Shenk, HarperSanFrancisco, San Francisco, 1997, ISBN: 0060187018

Are you amazed at the reams of information that new technologies have made available to you? A little overwhelmed by all the data you have to wade through to find what you're looking for? *Data Smog* author David Shenk knows how you feel. Shenk was infatuated with information technology—until he realized that he was being bombarded with too much information, so much that it was destroying his quality of life. He feels that we're moving toward an information-infested society of people with weakened vision, sore backs, and "culturally induced ADD" (attention deficit disorder). In *Data Smog*, Shenk declares that the information glut is causing problems such as social fragmentation, the breakdown of democracy, the decline of educational standards, and the empowerment of demagogues. Shenk frames the book with his 13 "Laws of Data Smog" (such as "Silicon circuits evolve much more quickly than human genes" and "Cyberspace is Republican") and proceeds to explain the truth behind each of these bold statements. At the end of the book, Shenk offers five antidotes for the problem, suggesting that people filter their own intake and output of information and even proposing that the government get involved in protecting consumers from information spam. For those who have experienced some kind of information overload, *Data Smog*—with its conversational style, personal anecdotes, and quotes from industry specialists—is mesmerizing.

Digital Literacy by Paul Gilster, John Wiley & Sons, New York, 1997, ISBN: 0471165204

With all the hyperbole being spouted by people on both sides of the digital technology fence, Paul Gilster's intelligent, sobering look at the Internet is a breath of fresh air. Gilster is obviously a champion of the Internet, but he exhibits just enough skepticism in *Digital Literacy* to let you know he's hardly a knee-jerk apologist for the digerati. Digital literacy is defined as "a way of reading and understanding information that differs from what we do when we sit down to read a book or a newspaper." The book's goal is to provide a means of understanding the information we receive on our computers. After all, we're living in an era in which "if you can think it, it can be digitized." The book analyzes titles written by a couple of famous Luddites: *The Gutenberg Elegies*, by Sven Birkert, and *Silicon Snake Oil*, by Clifford Stoll. While acknowledging the validity of some of their arguments, *Digital Literacy* calmly refutes their challenges that the Internet and digital technology devalue human interaction and literacy. The author mixes personal experience with solid research to offer a clear-minded approach for evaluating content received from the Internet. *Digital Literacy* is a fascinating look at the world of cyberspace and a good corrective for anyone who is starry-eyed about the information they find on-line.

Information Anxiety by Richard Saul Wurman, Doubleday, New York, 1990, ISBN: 0385243944

What is information anxiety? It's that nagging feeling that no matter how hard you try, you just can't keep up with everything going on around you. It's nodding your head knowingly when someone mentions a book or a movie you've never heard of. It's feeling depressed because you don't know what all the functions are for on your computer or VCR. It's panicking when you hear the Dow has dropped 500 points—even though you don't really know what that means. But most of all, it's being embarrassed to say simply "I don't know"! Wurman explains why the information explosion has backfired, leaving us stranded between mere facts and real understanding. He presents a more sensible way to handle the barrage of information we face every day. Using three easy-to-apply principles, Wurman shows us how to get the information we need and how to use it effectively. Even though this book is several years old, it's still right on the mark as it sets out all of the gory details of infowhelm and information overload and has been thoroughly researched.

Literacy in a Digital World: Teaching and Learning in the Age of Information by Kathleen Tyner, Lawrence Erlbaum Associates, Mahwah, NJ, 1998, ISBN: 0805822267

The growing prominence of electronic and digital media in communities and schools raises complex questions about the nature and consequences of literacy in a culturally diverse society. In education, emphasis on the cultivation of reading and writing skills has given way to a host of alternative conceptual, theoretical, and pedagogical approaches to literacy. This volume provides a clearly written overview of visual, informational, and media literacy and focuses on the authors and professional cultures associated with each of these subfields. It describes how each group has dealt with problems of representation and legitimization, emphasizing the need for cross-disciplinary and international collaboration and synthesis. The text also describes in detail how educators are using print, video, photographs, and computers to foster literacy, defined as "the ability to access, analyze, evaluate, and produce information." This volume will interest media educators and researchers, information specialists, teacher educators, and students seeking an introduction to the field and examples of how new technologies and literacy practices can be integrated into the elementary, secondary, and postsecondary curriculum.

Understanding Media: The Extensions of Man by Marshall McLuhan, MIT Press, Cambridge, MA, 1994, ISBN: 0262631598

This reissue marks the 30th anniversary (1964–1994) of McLuhan's classic exposé on the state of the emerging phenomenon of mass media. In a new introduction, Harper's editor Lewis Lapham reevaluates McLuhan's work in the light of the technological as well as the political and social changes that have occurred in the last part of the century.

Printed in the United States
By Bookmasters